THE ACCIDENTAL COUGAR

Top Ten Reasons Your Man
Has an Older Woman
on the Side

Susan Anderson, M.Ed.

Published in the United States
By ONE LIFE PUBLISHING

ISBN # 978-0-9838811-0-0

Copyright ©2011
by Susan Anderson

All rights reserved. This document, or parts thereof, may not be reproduced in any form – other than quotes for articles and reviews where credit is given – without written permission from Susan Anderson. All rights are also reserved for translation into foreign languages. No liability is assumed with respect to the information herein.

Dedication

To R.M., K.J., and M.S., who asked the right questions.

This book has been written for women whose partners are seeing older women, sometimes known as cougars. It is intended to help wives and girlfriends understand the appeal of the cougar and enable them to adjust their own behavior, if they choose, to make cougars an unnecessary part of their men's lives.

THE ACCIDENTAL COUGAR

Top Ten Reasons Your Man Has an Older Woman on the Side

Susan Anderson, M.Ed.

Table of Contents

1. Introduction 11
2. The Myth of the Cougar (or exactly who chased whom?) 21
3. So you think you're happily married... 35
4. Top ten reasons your man may have a cougar on the side 45
5. But he works two jobs! When does he have the time? 63

6	Circus sex?? (You may not want to know.) 73
7	The high-maintenance man 93
8	Sins of omission 105
9	How young? How old? 117
10	Strategies to find out if he is involved 129
11	Does anybody ever really own anybody? 139
12	Your options now that you know 149
13	Ten talks you must have with your man (or your *next* man) 161
14	What's in it for the cougar? 171
15	The sex your man wants 187
16	A Final Word 199

"Author Shere Hite claims that 70 percent of the women who have been married for more than five years engage in extramarital affairs. And she lets them off the hook by saying that those women are seeking something that is lacking in their married lives. Most men are in the same position. They are after emotional or sexual satisfaction and attention that is absent at home."

~ Bob Berkowitz, *What Men Won't Tell You But Women Need to Know*

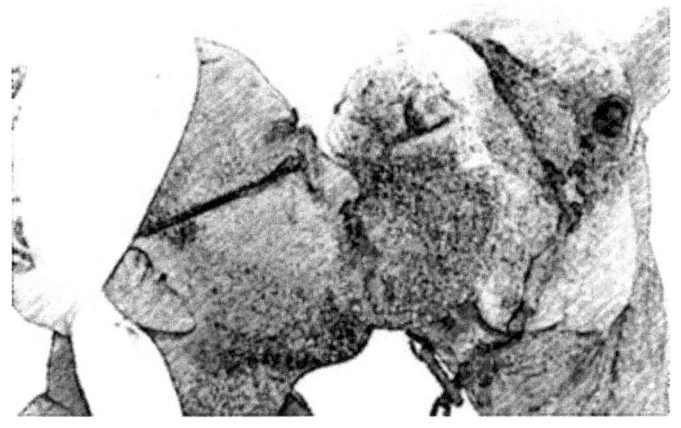

1 • Introduction

"My husband would *never* sleep with an old woman! He'd laugh at the very idea of such a thing! I'm much more worried about the frisky young things down at his gym. They're likely to pull down his zipper *for* him!"

That's the typical response of young wives (or girlfriends) when asked about the possibility of an older woman in their husbands' or boyfriends' lives. Well, girlfriend, this book is here to tell you that not only is the older woman – the cougar – a real possibility, but she may *already* be a regular part of your man's life.

This is probably not a book you ever visualized yourself even reading, much less needing. If you are in a relationship with a man, though, whether you are dating, exclusive, or married, you do need the information and insights you're about to acquire.

Men are different from women in many ways. That's a broad generalization, of course, but keep the "different" in mind as you read through these pages. They will explain why your man can do some things that you would find extremely hurtful and disloyal and yet think it's "no big thing." Knowing that men may look at a situation very differently from women can help you accept the truth and then decide how to proceed.

If you thought relationships were difficult yesterday, wait till you examine them today!

In this book, real-life cougars have volunteered information that women need to hear before they marry. Believe me, it's not easy to find actual cougars who are willing to talk about their experiences. Being "the other woman" under any circumstances is not usually an enviable position, nor anything to boast about. But today, the older woman has come under even more fire, from the media, from the pulpit, and from society at large, for her involvement with younger men. So to hear these women speak frankly about what they and their young men hope to get from their relationships is, at once, edifying, titillating, and genuinely concerning to us all. Unfortunately, most women – prior to marrying, at least – wouldn't accept this kind of information willingly. So it remains for those of you who are already married or in a serious relationship to get a proper heads-up on what can happen between your man and an older woman. We prefer to call it "preparing for the worst-case scenario," but alas it's all too common.

Remember, too, that times are changing. What society dictated for your mother's generation may not hold true today. We see evidence that fewer couples are marrying, choosing to live together instead. A growing number of "couples" maintain separate living spaces and just come together on weekends or several nights a week. The marriage bond appears to be weakening, or suffering from dilution at the very least.

Couples today are also having fewer, if any, children. Children are expensive and time-consuming, and they distract parents from being able to focus on their own needs. The world doesn't condemn couples for making the choice to remain childless the way it might have a generation or two ago.

Human beings have always lived in a time of flux, but the flux seems to be moving faster these days. Try not to judge your man or your relationship by standards that may be obsolete. That doesn't mean you can't have your own personal standards. You can and you should. So should he. But these need to be communicated clearly to one another, and we have found that frequently important information is left unsaid.

The older women whose stories and advice you will read here were once young, married women, perhaps like yourself. They entered into couplehood with high expectations and maybe a little bit of fantasy-thinking. They were all victims of their own naivete, ignorance, and tunnel vision (and often their partners' selfishness). All have since been divorced. But their cautionary tales may help you avoid the very pitfalls to which they succumbed in their early relationships with their significant others. At the very least, their stories will enable you to deal with your man with eyes wide open.

With fifty percent of first marriages ending in divorce and second marriages faring even more poorly, either we are doing something wrong or marriage has ceased to be a viable institution. Unfortunately, just living together doesn't work out any better than marriage and rarely leads to "forever after" in the long run. Perhaps the institution of marriage has run its course?

Our daughters and our friends' daughters will be facing a time in our history when a young woman's choice may no longer be between marriage-and-family or singlehood, but rather between bearing children outside of marriage or not bearing children at all. That's a conversation that some clear-sighted women are already having with their daughters. Who could have known it would ever come to that?

In *Manning Up: How the Rise of Women Has Turned Men into Boys,* Kay Hymowitz describes the many men in their 20s (and even some in their 30s) who live in an extended adolescence in colleges and grad schools prescribed by the needs of our "Knowledge Economy." That pre-adult stage may continue well into his 30s as a man works on developing his career at the expense of marrying and starting a family, the route his parents' generation took. When he is finally able to settle down and marry, he may wonder, "What for?" After all, he's been getting his needs met without marriage for so many years that marriage seems superfluous. A recent *Glamour* magazine article stated that today's young men expect *at least* a blow job by the third date. A man certainly doesn't have to be married to get it. Not that men have ever needed marriage to get sex, but these days it's awesomely easy to obtain. Poor Erik Erikson. He must be rolling over in his grave.

So is marriage obsolete? Not entirely, although other options appear more appealing to many men. Those who do marry in their mid- or late-20s tend to be more traditional types who have learned to value marriage and family life, perhaps because of their own reasonably happy families of origin. But make no mistake about it. Even men who choose marriage probably do not do so with the starry-eyed wonder that many young women do. Men, by and large, are practical creatures, and they will do what is best for *them* most of the time.

We are likely to see fewer marriages in the future as men decide that the likelihood of divorce and its financial consequences make the marriage pact a shaky proposition at best. We may, in fact, see dramatic changes in family configurations, both in this country and abroad, as a result of this apprehension regarding marriage. Some of these changes are already becoming evident in our culture: women raising children alone, men fleeing from commitment to both girlfriends and children, and cohabitation replacing marriage as the favored living arrangement.

This book is not based on stringent scientific sampling procedures or a broad base of respondent demographics. It's largely anecdotal. Finding the older "other woman" is not an easy task. There is no reason for her to want to talk about her experiences. In fact, most other women would rather not rock the boat at all. They are happy with their choices and would just as soon remain "a silent subculture." But the women who did volunteer to speak to us offer important information that should not be ignored by any wife or girlfriend. This book hopes to open your eyes to what attached men sometimes consider a "practical necessity" – a safe, satisfying, undemanding woman on the side. Who might that be? The cougar is the woman you're least likely to suspect.

Further Reading

Berkowitz, Bob (2008). *What Men Won't Tell You But Women Need to Know.* NY:Harper Collins Publishers.

Hymowitz, Kay S. (2011). *Manning Up: How the Rise of Women Has Turned Men into Boys.* NY: Basic Books.

Oh, Kara (1999). *Men Made Easy.* Beverly Hills: Avambre Press.

Unterberger, Lindsey (Sept. 2011). "And the #1 Thing He Wants in Bed Is...." *Glamour* Magazine.

"Yeah, I cheat. Look at my wife. Wouldn't you?"

~ From a cheater's blog

Straight from the Cougar's Mouth:

"I see him about twice a week. I don't know how often he's sleeping with his girlfriend, but I guess it's not often enough. Maybe she doesn't realize how much he needs it."

"Men are motivated primarily by two things — money and sex."

~ David M. Matthews, *Every Man Sees You Naked: An Insider's Guide to How Men Think*

2 • The Myth of the Cougar

(or, exactly who chased whom?)

If we believed everything we read on the internet, we would rush home right now and lock up our men to keep them safe from cougars. Cougars? You know. The older women who prey on young men? Yeah. THOSE cougars.

In the 1967 movie, *The Graduate*, Anne Bancroft became the quintessential prototype for all cougars who would later follow in her footsteps. And she certainly was a tough act to follow: slim and lovely and positively dripping with sex appeal. In the film, of course, she pursued young Benjamin Braddock (Dustin Hoffman), establishing the ground rules for the official definition of *cougar*: **Cougar** refers to an older woman, usually in her 30s-40s (or older), who sexually pursues younger men in their 20s or 30s *(from Wikipedia.org)*.

Some of us have always hoped that Anne reveled in her cougar status, enjoying every delicious reference to Mrs. Robinson, right up to the day she died. She deserved it. She *was* the prototypical American cougar. The rest of us women can take some small comfort if our men are targeted by such a stunning and irresistible predator as Anne Bancroft. After all, who *wouldn't* succumb to her charms? But these days, let's be honest, the cougar may be less the pursuer and more the pursued.

Even in the dating world of the third millennium, the male of the species still claims the most prerogatives: he can initiate a conversation, he can ask for that first date, he can continue the relationship as long as he chooses to do so, he can terminate the relationship whenever he wishes, or he can propose a seemingly more committed relationship, such as moving in together or even marriage. A woman who usurps these male prerogatives may tend to come off as too aggressive, too man-like. Not good for the male ego, therefore not likely to be good for the woman. The woman, of course, has the right to refuse a man's advances. However, as the relationship-nurturer, a woman may sometimes even continue to date a guy for a while out of a sense of kindness, because he's been so nice to her, while looking for a way to let him down gently. Or she may initiate "the talk," in which she spells out, sorry, sorry, sorry, how she just doesn't have the same feelings for him that he has for her.

Don't kid yourself. There's usually no "talk" for the male of the species. If the guy loses interest first, the relationship is over. OVER. Even if they haven't discussed it. Pffffft. Over. Remember that guy you dated for six months? The last time you saw him, he cooked corned beef and cabbage for you on St. Patrick's Day? And then suddenly – nothing. A disappearing act David Copperfield would be proud of. He just dropped off the radar one day, never to be heard from again. Or the doctor? A whole summer of concerts, dinners, and picnics under the stars? Alas, one day, no more doctor. (You know he didn't die – you checked his hospital's website and he's still working there.) "Sudden and total disappearance" seems to be the classic break-up protocol that men learn very early in their dating lives. Love 'em, then leave 'em. A cold summary, perhaps, but one based on a great many real-life occurrences. (The cougars we spoke to said men terminate their relationships with cougars in much the same brutal fashion. Older, more mature men do the same. We surmise it's a guy thing, based on a reluctance to admit unnecessary "drama" into their lives.)

Women tend to be serial monogamists while dating, limiting themselves to one man at a time while they assess his potential as a long-term partner. Men seldom do the same. Based on the argument that they are, after all, *not married yet*, or even engaged, men will date several women at a time, enjoying a variety of personalities, looks, and sexual styles. And it is into this mix that the cougar often finds herself added.

Contrary to what magazines and a few books would have us believe, the cougar is not always a predator. She is more likely to be an older woman who actually has difficulty meeting available men her own age and hasn't seriously thought about seeing a younger man until – one day – a younger man approaches *her*. His overture may actually surprise and confuse her until she's had time to mull it over. Deciding to try some kind of May-December relationship was probably not her idea at all, but his. However, in the absence of any older prospects, she often thinks, *What the hell. Why not?* And thus an affair begins.

So if it's not the older woman who preys on a younger man, then how do we explain a younger man pursuing someone a decade or more his senior? Simply put, because he can. One young man put it even more bluntly: "Opportunism. If the opportunity presents itself, and I have the time, I take it." Another, whose words probably sum up many a man's feelings, volunteered, "I never get enough sex. Having a woman on the side is exactly what I needed."

Smith and Doe, in their now-classic guide, *What Men Don't Want Women to Know: The Secrets, the Lies, the Unspoken Truth,* point out that a man who turns down an opportunity to have sex with another woman "berates himself daily for having acted like a weak-minded idiot." The authors go on to say he will make damn sure that he doesn't make that same mistake twice.

Once a young man finds himself attracted to a particular older woman (because of her mind, her body, her availability, or his own curiosity), it is only a matter of time before he will make his move. Unless he is extremely shy and withdrawn, he *will* proposition her. The when, where, and how may not yet be clear to him, but the intention to enter into some kind of relationship with this woman definitely is. Yes, your man is an opportunist.

Most young men want or need more sex than their girlfriends or wives are willing to give them. A man may, indeed, have married the woman of his dreams, but once she stopped craving sex three times a day, every day, on the hood of his car, between the library stacks, and in the elevator, he took off the rose-colored glasses. Reality kicked in. Suddenly, every woman on the planet once again became fair game. Now, that doesn't mean the young man is ready to dump his girl. No, he'll just have to find a way – discreetly – to supplement the amount of sex he gets from her. And the older woman can fill that void quite nicely.

Generally speaking, men who aren't seriously handicapped or disfigured in some way will adamantly refuse to visit a prostitute. (That decision will likely change when a guy gets older and discovers that finding interested women can be too exhausting, too time-consuming, or just plain futile.) To a young man, paying for sex implies that he cannot attract a woman on his own merits, and that does an awful number on his ego. So what remains is this: throughout his days and weeks, *your man begins to size up every woman he comes into contact with* and tries to determine what chance he has of sleeping with her. That's right. *Every woman.* Even women you would never suspect. The women at his office, his neighbors, the clerks at WalMart, the personal trainers at his gym. Your sister, your best friend, his own mother's best friend. It sounds insane, but all these women are processed through the young man's brain in a methodical fashion. If they're female, they'll be sized up. And then he'll begin hitting on the ones that he suspects or hopes might be receptive.

"Not my husband!" you shriek. But think about it. How much sex do you two really have? Not as much or as often as you used to. And are there certain things that you know he wants (well, he wanted them in the past) but that you don't like to do? Guess what? He's getting his surplus sex and his "kinky" sex from another woman. Maybe an older woman. A cougar.

So why an older woman? There are plenty of reasons, but perhaps the most obvious one is that the older woman is safe in so many ways that a younger woman is not. She probably can't get pregnant, she doesn't want to marry your guy, she's discreet, and she's thoroughly uninhibited and unembarrassed about sexual activities. Plus, she's thought it through. Their no-strings-attached relationship suits her just fine. And of course it suits your guy too.

Sex, according to psychologist Kevin Leman, does a lot for a man. It's energizing, confidence-building, and enhances his sense of well-being. He craves it. If you turn your man's advances down, he WILL pay you back. Even saying something as innocent (and truthful) as, "Honey, I can't. The kids were just awful today, and I'm exhausted!" is enough, in a man's book, to warrant looking elsewhere. And even if you do indulge him, frequently and with enthusiasm, there's still that thrill of the chase and the excitement of doing something forbidden that will tempt him to cross that line.

Nina met a young American doctor of East Indian descent who was engaged to a woman who was finishing her J.D. degree. She was also from the same ethnic background. What this young man wanted was something his liberated American bride-to-be wouldn't do: he wanted a totally submissive woman who would behave much like a slave or concubine and follow his every instruction. We can imagine what his girlfriend, just completing her law degree, probably thought of that idea. So, for a couple of years, Dr. Raj met with Nina who played along with his desires. Nina says she enjoyed it immensely, and it didn't hurt that he was extremely well-endowed. (Well, maybe a little.)

There are also specific times in the life of a marriage (or relationship) that put extra stress on the couple. During those times it is highly likely that your man will seek out the comforting arms of another woman, perhaps a cougar. Be especially wary during when:

- You're pregnant and uncomfortable.
- You're dealing with a huge job problem, or he is, such as being fired or demoted.
- You're moving, and much of the planning falls on you.
- Either of your parents are ill, or undergoing medical treatment, or facing some life stress that requires your assistance.

- Either of you is ill or in need of medical treatment.
- A death in either of your families-of-origin requires time away from home.
- A legal situation is causing one or both of you distress.
- Your residence is disrupted by the presence of a relative or friend who needs to live with you temporarily.
- Children are requiring more and more of your attention and the household is becoming increasingly child-centered and noisy.
- Your child is diagnosed with a learning disability or other handicap.
- Almost *any* other stress-producing event. (Remember: for men, sex is the stress-reliever of choice.)

Other cultures have sanctioned secret mistresses or other women for eons, as long as no embarrassment or humiliation fell to the wife. Americans are less likely to overtly prescribe an affair as a marital salve. But, covertly, many men have come to accept the cougar as the lesser of two evils. Since she doesn't want to take him away from his wife or girlfriend, she is less dangerous than a younger woman looking for a husband for herself. And the cougar won't "accidentally" get pregnant and make him her baby daddy. Nevertheless, most women find sharing a man with another woman in any fashion admittedly difficult or impossible to contemplate.

Today, a new perspective on the older woman may be called for. Rather than view her unquestionably as a predator, wives and girlfriends should examine from where the impetus for the affair came. Most likely, the man himself made the initial overture. Simply exacting a promise from him to stop seeing her does not address the underlying question of what made him seek out another partner at all. What needs or wants was he hoping to fulfill? Is there something his wife or girlfriend can do to rectify the situation? While not all men feel troubled by stepping outside their primary relationship, some do and would like to resolve matters.

If you suspect your man is involved with an older woman, or *any* woman, you need to sit down and sort out some issues, probably with a disinterested third party such as a psychologist or marital counselor. While life doesn't always fall into neat little boxes, an enlightened professional can often show the way to saving a relationship by pointing out the tweaks that are necessary to allow it to work for both parties involved.

Further Reading

Block, Joel D. & Kimberly Dawn Neumann (2009). *Sex Comes First: Fifteen Ways to Save Your Relationship ... without leaving your bedroom.* Avon, MA:Adams Media.

Leman, Kevin (2007). *7 Things He'll Never Tell You (But You Need to Know).* Carol Stream, IL: Tyndale House.

"According to eminent marriage therapist John Gottman, 67% of married couples have a precipitous drop in relationship happiness in the first three years of their baby's life."

> ~ Ian Kerner,
> *Love in the Time of Colic*

Straight from the Cougar's Mouth:

"Actually, I wish I were 30 again. I would go after him myself. His wife must not know what a catch he is, or he wouldn't be here with me."

> *"The only reason your man is with you is because, at this moment in time, he genuinely believes he simply can't do any better."*
>
> ~ Smith and Doe in *What Men Don't Want Women to Know: The Secrets, the Lies, the Un-Spoken Truth*

3 • So You Think You're Happily Married...

All of us had parents. However happy or unhappy their relationship was, we women vowed that our marriage would be better. We would work harder to make it so. And when we met the man we wanted to spend our lives with, we took it for granted that he would work just as hard.

But maybe marriage wasn't his dream. Maybe his dream had more to do with carving out a career that he could be proud of, or simply making that first million. Maybe he had visions of traveling around the world, or competing in sailing regattas. Oh, he wanted you in his life, for sure, but over time, your dreams crowded out his dreams, and he's felt cheated. Did you want a certain kind of house, and he let you have your way? Did you both want children? At the same time? Or did you one day find yourself pregnant and that's how your family began? It didn't seem like a big deal at the time, perhaps, but as months and years went by, your man felt deprived of his dreams and resented that. Stuff was happening to him that wasn't in his plans. Maybe he's always wanted to live in New York, but you couldn't bear to be that far away from your family. Or he imagined the two of you living simply, and somehow your needs outpaced your incomes and you both became slaves to a lifestyle that wasn't of his choosing. In some way, he (consciously or unconsciously) became determined to even the score.

Your being a good partner and/or mother is just not enough for your guy. If he has theoretically given up intimate encounters with other women for you, he's probably missing something. Plus, his reputation among his peers is in jeopardy. They judge him by the beer he drinks, the job he holds, and the women he beds. If you don't impress them, he will know it, and he will need to save face somehow. Are you attractive enough to merit their approval? Do you treat him like a man in front of them? Is he getting from you the sexual satisfaction they've all agreed they would never settle for less than? If a relationship were just between the two of you, how much simpler things would be! But you know how you must answer to your girlfriends concerning him. Well, he has to answer to his buds.

Depending on who his friends are, they may actually encourage a cheating lifestyle as a sign of manliness. Left to himself, your man might never stray, but with friends who want to out-do one another on the manliness scale, it's tough for a guy to opt out. Of course, the responsibility still lies with the man himself, but peer pressure is powerful at all ages.

Many men also see having a woman on the side as the ultimate "get even" strategy. There's a smugness in their attitude which says, "The wife got me to give up my hobby (sailing, motorcycles, fishing with my buddies), but wouldn't she just shit if she knew I was fucking Alice when she thought I was at Benjamin Moore looking at paint?" The relationship with the cougar gives him an edge over you, even though you may know nothing about it.

Once a man is deeply invested in your relationship (you own property together, or you have children, or all his and your friends see you as a couple), he may find it difficult to ask for what he needs. What he needs can be anything from embarrassingly kinky sex to more time without the kids around, but if the two of you have fallen into a behavioral pattern that doesn't speak to those needs, then he must either deny them or satisfy them surreptitiously. This is where the cougar often comes in.

A woman your own age is too dangerous. She may be looking for a long-term partner herself, in which case she will pressure your guy to leave you. Or she might contact you in an effort to have you leave him. She can become pregnant, she can hassle him at work, and she can demand more of his time than he is capable of giving her. But a cougar presents none of these problems. She looks like the perfect solution to his quandary - "Why don't I ever get what *I* want?" - without complicating matters further.

We've all heard the admonition that good communication is the key to a successful relationship, but we don't actually apply it. After a couple of years together, people learn what topics to avoid if they don't want to instigate an argument. That's probably what's happened to you and your guy. You no longer talk about touchy subjects (if you ever did) because you or he are afraid of the anger or bad feelings that might follow. So your man goes behind your back to get what he thinks he needs.

Marriage is a much more complicated arrangement than most people want to admit. Especially in the West, we are conditioned to think that as long as there is love, love will conquer all. Love *can* overcome many obstacles, but careful planning and thorough discussion ahead of the marriage is still essential. (See chapter 13 for some of the conversations you should be having *before* the wedding.)

Gary Neuman, author of *The Truth about Cheating: Why Men Stray and What You Can Do to Prevent It,* surveyed hundreds of cheating and faithful husbands to find out why men cheat on their wives. Ninety-two percent of the cheaters said it wasn't about the sex. The majority said it was an emotional disconnection – a sense of feeling underappreciated. And while that may well be true, just how *do* men measure their wives' appreciation? By the frequency and quality of the sex they get at home. As Smith and Doe say, "He's not with you because you make a bangin' beef stroganoff." He's with you for the sex. If he's given up other women (monogamy!), then the sex had better be good.

Think about it. Women's magazines are always telling us not to wait for husbands or boyfriends to tell us how they feel or to express verbally their love and appreciation for us. Men have trouble saying the L word. We're supposed to observe how they act and determine their feelings based on their actions. So if your guy is cleaning the gutters and helping with the laundry, you should feel pretty secure that he's a happy camper.

Now turn that concept around and imagine what the verbally-challenged guy is thinking, based on his wife's behavior. He's watching her and notices that she spends a lot of time driving the kids around to school and to playdates, She's taking her mom to dialysis several times a week and helping to clean her house. Twice a week she takes an evening class, working toward her master's degree so that she can go back to work some day when the kids are more self-sufficient. And once in a great while, when she's not too tired, she'll have sex with her man. Not crazy, the-neighbors-are-going-to-call-the-police sex, but your garden variety missionary position sex. Yep. He feels *real* underappreciated. For men, sex *is* emotional connection. Some women need to be hit over the head with this concept before they get it.

We women frequently do crazy, self-defeating things without realizing it. There are too many married men who can confide, quite honestly, that their wives have unilaterally decided how much sex they're going to have, or whether they're even going to have sex at all. (That's right: there's even a growing awareness among therapists of the large numbers of married couples who no longer have sex at all. Or have it so infrequently that it doesn't even compute. Alarmingly, these couples aren't all in the geriatric category. The husbands may not even have been given a chance to vote on the issue. And they're *not* happy.)

Those of us who have been divorced know full well the horrendous toll (emotionally, socially, and financially) that divorce exacts from the couple and their immediate families. When one partner is unhappy in the relationship, divorce begins to loom ominously on the horizon as a viable option. That is why both husband and wife need to check in, honestly, with each other on a regular basis to detect areas of their life together that may need repair.

On the surface, and to their friends, many marriages look just fine. But if there is a cougar in the picture, things are not as fine as they seem. A man may have a great deal invested in his relationship or family and doesn't wish to leave, but he is still an individual who has specific wants and needs. If you suspect that your partner is seeing someone on the side, then your relationship is not an honest one. You must find a way to bring up this issue and talk about it. A counselor or psychologist might be the right third party to help you both examine what is going on and how your relationship might be repaired. Certainly if there are children involved, this is a step you both must take.

Can every relationship be repaired? No. But you won't know if yours can be until you sit down and talk it out. Calmly.

Interestingly, Anne had a relationship of several years with a man whose wife divorced him when she found out he was cheating with someone else. Through some of the female insights that Anne was able to convey to him, Dan admitted that he really just wanted to get back together with his wife and just didn't know how to go about it. He had fucked up and he knew it. Anne helped him to put together a plan, and Dan and his wife are now dating again. He no longer sees Anne, but he calls her every few weeks to report on his progress! Because the cougar doesn't allow herself to become emotionally involved with the younger man, she can remain friends with him even after their relationship has ended.

Further Reading

Neuman, M. Gary (2008). *The Truth about Cheating: Why Men Stray and What You Can Do to Prevent It.* Hoboken, NJ:John Wiley & Sons.

Smith and Doe (1998). *What Men Don't Want Women to Know: The Secrets, the Lies, the Unspoken Truth.* NY: St. Martin's Press.

"Seriously though, if you want a sure fire way to spice things up in bed, give him good head! Not a guy on the planet (gay or straight!) doesn't want good head!"

~ Justin, from Yahoo!Answers

"I do not think about sex every 20 seconds. More like every 15."

~ From a man's profile on Adultfriendfinder.com.

4 • Top Ten Reasons Your Man Has a Cougar on the Side

It's 10:00 pm. Janet has just finished putting her two young sons to bed and sits down on the sofa to catch the news. Between caring for the kids and overseeing her dad's hospitalization, it's been an exhausting day. Before the commercials are finished, she's sound asleep. Unconscious is a better word.

Her husband, Rich, comes in from the kitchen where he has been working on their income taxes. Seeing his wife asleep on the sofa, he knows his hopes for a little fun at bedtime are going to be dashed. When she's that tired, there's no way he's going to talk her into sex. So he goes into the bathroom, locks the door, and calls Anne on his cell. Oh, well, he sighs, as her phone rings. Phone sex is better than no sex. And it's better than solo sex, too. Plus, Anne won't plead tired. She's always up for talking dirty. He'll get off.

She's not rich. She's probably not beautiful. And, jeez, she's old enough to be his mother! She couldn't possibly be a threat to your relationship, could she? Hmmmmm. Better think again. Sometimes, danger lurks in places we would never suspect.

You know the usual warning: Men just can't help looking at an attractive young woman. And for the most part that's true. Mother Nature, according to anthropologist Helen Fisher, programs the male of the species to seek out young, healthy, fertile females. So you monitor your man's gaze at parties and restaurants, and when you think he's scoped out enough nubile young beauties, you treat him to an elbow jab to the ribs. That's enough, buster.

But men also know there are some distinct advantages for a guy who welcomes the older female, sometimes pejoratively termed "cougar," into his life. As a young wife or girlfriend, you should make a point of familiarizing yourself with the reasons why your man might turn to an older woman occasionally (or regularly!) for sex and companionship and decide how you will deal with that issue if and when it arises. While it's probably not something you relish thinking about, forewarned can definitely be forearmed.

Most cougars learned these lessons the hard way – through shocking revelations when they were themselves married. You don't have to learn that way. But you'd better listen up now.

1. **The older woman can't get pregnant** (or, if she can, she is verrrry careful about birth control). Think about the guys you know who carelessly got their girlfriends pregnant and then either married them quickly or at least began paying the first installments of eighteen years of child support.

   This situation is not confined to any social class. Even celebrities have "baby daddies." Linda Evangelista just watched her boyfriend – one of the richest men in the world – marry Salma Hayek. Both women bore him children within a year of one another! So, having lost out in the marriage race, Linda's going after a level of child support that most of us would consider an outright hallucination. The tabloids put the figure at $46,000 a month.

   But back to reality. After the dust settles and our average guys sit down to review WTF happened, they realize that birth control is largely or totally under the woman's control, unless the guy uses a condom religiously (LOL), and we all know that isn't going to happen any time soon. Whether a real pregnancy or just a missed period scared the bejabbers out of a guy, suddenly the older woman with no more ovulations to worry about starts looking like a pretty good alternative. Guys who already have children can appreciate the bleak reality that their children's needs will always come first with their wives or girlfriends. Bummer.

> *The cougar thinks you should know:*
> *"Having babies is a wonderful thing, but that's a woman's drive, not a man's. Most of the men I've known have only gone along with it because their wives wanted children – including my own husband. Now a man's most persistent drive is sex. Once a woman gets what she wants – a baby – she often forgets all about her man's drive. That's what I've found."*

2. **The older woman doesn't want to get married.** At least not to your guy. She's probably been there, done that, and is just looking for an attractive, occasional sex partner, just like your guy is. If she ever does marry again, it will probably be to someone in her own generational demographic. (Apologies to Demi and Ashton.) So there is little chance of relationship

pressure, hardly any of those "we need to talk" talks, and the older woman doesn't even expect your guy to introduce her to his friends and family. It may be nothing more than a casual sexual relationship, which is exactly what he wants from her. If they can also have intelligent conversations about art or world events, so much the better.

> *The cougar thinks you should know: "He sometimes brings your baby to my place if he's babysitting. Or your dog, if they've been out for a walk. Yep."*

3. **The older woman never looks too shabby.** She won't let your man see her without a fresh manicure or clean hair. No grungy sweats when he comes over. And never when she's got the flu. She's had some cosmetic surgeries over the years, so she probably doesn't look like your typical middle-aged woman. She works out regularly, something you may have stopped doing just before your second child came along, and she eats healthy. She knows the power of a smile, and she always has one for him. Not only does she smell good between the sheets, but she always smells good. Sometimes your man has to shower before he comes home to you so he doesn't smell just like her.

The older woman knows that getting a boyfriend or a husband is not the end of the game. *Keeping him* may be just as much work, or more, than catching him was. Unfortunately, women can never afford to let their guards down when it comes to attractiveness. Nope. Never. Not even after five kids and a promise of "till death do us part." Just ask Eddie Murphy's ex.

> ***The cougar thinks you should know:***
> *"He's had me over to your home while you're at work or out of town. In your bed! Now that takes balls, right? It's obvious he knows your every move, if he can pull that off. You're too predictable."*

4. **The older woman may be up for more sexual experimentation than you are.** Your man can do anything he wants with his older woman that he does with you (and he will – so visualize *that* for a moment). But he can also ask his older woman to visit a sex club with him (so he can fulfill that long-held MFF fantasy) or let him dress up in women's lingerie. She'll do it. She's been with a lot of men, and she knows they can't help what they desire. Typically, men develop more fetishes than women, according to sex experts. So what's on the menu? Lick and

slurp his ass? Pee in his mouth? Tie him to the bed and spank him with a ping pong paddle? Why not? She's heard it all before, it won't kill her, and she knows he's got to have it. If not with her, then surely with someone else.

> ***The cougar thinks you should know:***
> *"We often do the things he says are taboo for you. Anal sex. Threesomes and double penetration. Rimming. Female domination. Think about any sex act you don't like to do. He's doing that one with me."*

5. **The older woman is *not* out to change him.** We've all heard that a man marries a woman for what she is today and hopes she'll never change, while a woman marries a man for the potential she sees in him, and then sets out to turn that potential into reality. Well, News Flash! Guys are generally pretty happy with who they are, and they don't appreciate being viewed as a "makeover project."

The older woman accepts your man with all his flaws (of course, she doesn't have to live with them fulltime). She doesn't ask him to change a thing. That kind of pressure doesn't exist in her world. He can be himself, all the time, when he's with her. As far as the cougar is concerned, he's okay just the way he is. This may stand in stark contrast to the way your man perceives *you*: always nagging him to change something about himself.

> ***The cougar thinks you should know:** "Once in a while, I'll meet him at a buddy's place. I've met a couple of his friends, the ones he can trust. They know about me even though you don't."*

6. **The older woman gives your man a perverse sense of control over you.** Not intentionally, of course, but that's the net effect. Let's say you and he have an argument and go to bed angry. No sex tonight, right? Well, hell. He'll show you. He can have sex any time he wants it if he has an older woman on the side. Chances are pretty good she'll be up for it too. And you won't suspect a thing. Or let's say you insist on spending Christmas week at your parents' home in Buffalo, even though you know he'll occupy most of that time helping your dad shovel tons of snow. The last person he'll see before you leave, and the first person he'll see when you return, is – that's right – his older woman. Kinda makes you wonder if you should *ever* force a man to do something he'd rather not.

If you two go without sex for a week, you can be pretty sure he's getting it somewhere else. Unlike the men in *Lysistrata*, your man does have someone who'll sleep with him. Ever catch that smug look on his face? The one that says, "I can go without it as long as you can"? Mmm hmm. Someone's not going without a thing.

> ***The cougar thinks you should know:** "I can always tell when you two are fighting. The frequency of his calls increases. The sex is more like a man on a mission too. I believe there's a strong element of 'getting even' in it."*

7. **Men love variety, but they don't want to destroy their current relationship to get it.** That's right. They want to have their cake and eat it too. Guys frequently put off commitment because they can't imagine having sex with only one woman for the rest of their lives. The older woman, even though she's not as physically attractive as you may be, allows your guy to experience that macho feeling of having multiple women at his beck and call. He does it because he can.

He's not really trying to hurt you, but he can't deny that he gets off on having a different woman now and then. A younger woman is too dangerous. After all, she may want to keep him for herself and decide to insert herself into your lives in some unpleasant way. The older woman won't do that. She's only in this for the occasional pleasure, and she won't jeopardize his relationship with you. (The older woman also realizes that she may not be the *only* other woman in the picture, and that doesn't bother her. She *will* use protection, even though your guy will beg and plead that she not.)

> **The cougar thinks you should know:** "He occasionally takes a half day off work so that he can be with me for a couple of hours. You'd only know that if you called him through the office switchboard, which you never do, because his cell phone is so much quicker. More than once he's answered your call at my place in the middle of a blowjob."

8. **The older woman probably wants sex with him more than you do.** Maybe because she doesn't have a man fulltime like you do, or maybe because her kids are grown and her life has settled into an unexciting routine, she appreciates the sex that she gets a lot more. Since she doesn't have the day-to-day reality issues with your man that you do, she always finds

him sexy. He may well be *very* sexy, a fact that you've forgotten over time.

And women's sex drives are not always compatible with men's. You may find yourself saying, "Not tonight," several times a week. After all, the baby's been sick and work is such a bitch. You're worn out. But if your guy likes it every day, don't kid yourself. He's going to find a way to get it. It may be with an older woman who accepts his overtures more willingly than you do. Not fair! Of course not. But, for him, sex is an inelastic demand.

> ***The cougar thinks you should know:*** *"A man considers sex a vital necessity, much like food or oxygen. If you don't share it with him as much or as often as he wants, he feels perfectly justified – JUSTIFIED! – coming to me or someone else for it. He really doesn't see that as morally wrong. It's only a problem if you find out."*

9. **The older woman may actually understand men better than you do.** She's known more of them than you have, at many different stages in their lives. One thing she's learned is that men are world-class compartmentalizers. Women are not. When a man is "doing it," that's all he wants to do. He doesn't want to be

reminded about work, or bills, or that unfortunate incident with the neighbors. The older woman respects this "guy thing." She doesn't ask your guy questions that make him uncomfortable. She doesn't broach topics that he's obviously unwilling to entertain. She keeps sex separate from the other "compartments" in his life.

She's also generous with compliments, telling him how good he looks and how much he satisfies her, even comparing him (favorably, of course!) to other men she's been with. The time he spends with her is all about *his* ego. The older woman knows that sex-time is about pleasure, not solving world problems.

The cougar thinks you should know:
"Although some of our meetings are spur-of-the moment, many are set up well in advance to take advantage of work holidays or dates when you will be out of town or otherwise engaged. Remember that weekend you spent with your old college roommates and he stayed home? Uh huh. We even did it while you were at your grandmother's funeral. If you remember, he said he couldn't get that day off work. Well, he did."

10. The older woman often serves as a retreat, a respite, from all that you represent. Yes, your guy chose you and the life you share. No, he doesn't want to be with any other woman more than with you. He's not leaving. But sometimes, for gosh sakes, he believes he deserves a friggin' break. Life is tough and he just wants to get away from his responsibilities for an hour or two. No explanations, no repercussions. Nothing but sheer, unadulterated (no pun intended) pleasure. Just pretend he's not even married for a while. A wife has a hard time understanding that.

The older woman's home is quiet, comfortable, and different from your home. Not better, just different. There's no drama. It serves as a getaway for a guy who feels that the pressures of living and working sometimes become too great. In that peculiar sort of "guy logic," he convinces himself that he's *earned* this couple of hours of stress relief. And he truly believes that what you don't know won't hurt you (or the relationship) in the long run.

Because we women are so into "sharing," your guy knows your schedule and when he can safely fly under your radar. It's pretty easy for him to slip away for a couple of hours.

> ***The cougar thinks you should know:***
> *"He gets off on the idea of having sex with two different women in the same day – me and you. It makes him feel self-satisfied in a caveman sort of way. Your guy has a lot of kinks he doesn't tell you about because he knows you'd freak if he did."*

Remember that almost no man is immune to the appeal of another woman – not former presidents, nor world-renowned religious leaders, not even your own father or brother. What's important for you to understand is what your man may be doing and *why* he's doing it. Only then can you determine how you will deal with the situation. You may want to get counseling, you may want to end the relationship, or, like some women, you may decide to allow his behavior to continue so long as it doesn't disrupt your life. You can even try to provide at home what he's been missing.

But one thing is certain: sticking your head in the sand and insisting that this isn't happening won't make the facts disappear. You must confront this issue the way you would confront any other problem in your relationship. (An excellent book on the topic of men and affairs is *Why Men Have Affairs*, by Irwin M. Marcus. All men are not alike, but you may find your particular man and his motivations among the types Dr. Marcus describes.)

Of course, you hope this will never happen to you, but armed with some information, you're now in a better position to avert the problem or deal with it constructively. As always, girlfriend, knowledge *is* power.

Further Reading

Berman, Laura, M.D. (2011) "Link Seen between Cheating & Anxiety."
http://www.suntimes.com/lifestyles/berman/6770813-452/link-seen-between-cheating-anxiety.html

Blanchard, Paul (1995). *Why Men Cheat and What to Do about It*. New York: Luv Books.

Marcus, Irwin (2004). *Why Men Have Affairs*. New Orleans: Bon Temps Press.

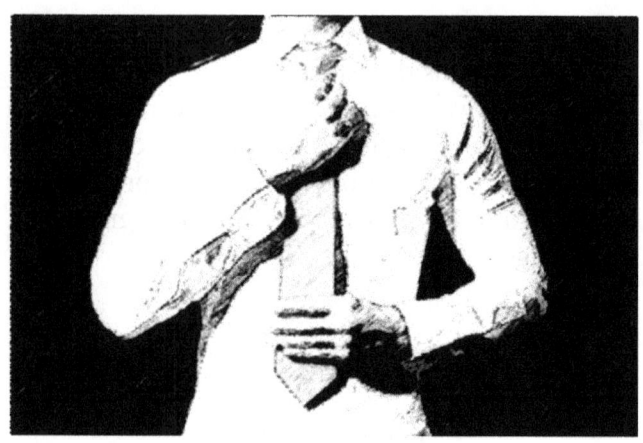

Nine Things You Need to Know about Your Guy:

1
He finds many kinds of female bodies attractive besides yours.

2
He needs sex much more often than he will admit.

3
He is more likely to lie than you are if it gets him what he wants and needs.

4
When he's not with you, he may not be where he said he would be.

5
His guy friends are a huge influence on him. Be sure you know them.

6
He wishes you could be everything he wants in a woman,, but you are not.

7
He's not as anxious to start a family as you are. It scares him.

8
He wishes he could be with several different women without anyone feeling hurt.

9
Sometimes he just wants to get away from you and think. Or just have incredible sex that no one would find out about.

Ask Yourself:

- **Has he ever asked me for some sex act that I denied him because I thought it was too disgusting?**
- **Do I sometimes nag or berate him as if I were his boss or his mother?**
- **Does our life together lack the excitement and spontaneity that it used to have?**
- **Does he carry a condom in his wallet or briefcase?**

> *"For men, cheating isn't always about sex. It's about all the excitement, romance, danger, and intrigue that surround it."*
>
> ~ David Zinczenko,
> *Men, Love & Sex*

5 • But He Works Two Jobs! When Does He Have the Time?

Sylvia's Story

Eric finished his computations for the presentation he had to make the next evening. He put everything in his briefcase, then headed toward the bedroom. Lisa was already sound asleep, quietly snoring. He shot off a brief text message, then quickly scribbled a note for Lisa on the bedside pad, in case she woke up and found him gone: *Shit! Forgot my notes at the office! Gotta drive over and get them. Be right back. Don't miss me too much!*

Then he let himself out to the carport and drove straight toward Sylvia's place.

The internet has opened up a great many new places to meet people. Dating sites, fetish clubs, Craigslist, topical chat rooms – all these provide new opportunities for your man to talk with and ultimately meet new women. But, perhaps not surprisingly, the most common place for a man to find a lover is right at work. In reviewing the chapters for this book, it suddenly became obvious that all the cougars who were sharing their stories had met at least some of their young men at work.

Maybe because it's easier to meet someone there than online, maybe because he gets the chance to observe the woman in question for weeks or even months before making his approach, or maybe because he already has a working relationship of some sort with her, the fact remains that the workplace is still the most likely environment where your man will meet the cougar with whom he becomes involved.

Men with flexible work schedules (CEOs, real estate brokers, salesmen, any men who travel frequently) find it easier to arrange meetings with other women than men who work a regular nine-to-five. But don't let that fool you! The very men who you think wouldn't have the time for an affair are often the ones who do. They are skilled at budgeting their time and working within a calendar, and, remember, a man can always take a half-day or a day off without telling his significant other. Meeting a woman on the side is not nearly as difficult as it may seem.

One young man told his older woman that "girls tell guys *everything* that they're doing, even stuff we don't want or need to know." Armed with that much information about your day or week, it's not difficult for him to set up something on the side. Men *definitely* do not tell women everything that's going on in their lives. They play their cards close to their vest. More about that in chapter 8.

Sylvia met her young man at work. They were both teachers at an elementary school and worked together for about five years before an affair began. They had been friendly, of course, but not particularly close. She taught eighth grade language arts; Eric was the gym teacher. But they saw one another every day and got to know each other as colleagues. Eventually they both moved on to other schools. Eric took a second job, part time, in real estate, where he hoped to get rich.

It wasn't until Eric saw Sylvia's profile on a dating website that he contacted her. In fact, he pursued her for a year before she agreed to see him. She kept telling him that the difference in their ages was too great. But Eric wouldn't be deterred. Finally, admitting to herself that he *was* attractive and she *was* flattered by his interest, Sylvia agreed to hook up with Eric.

Their first meeting was at his apartment, which he shared, at the time, with a male roommate who was gone for the evening. It was exciting, and the age difference actually added to the sexual tension between the two, because the relationship seemed somewhat taboo. That meeting led to many more: ten years, in fact, of regular weekly sexual encounters.

Eric sometimes had a girlfriend during those years, but that didn't stop him from seeing Sylvia. He always told her that she gave the best head he'd ever had, and he was very comfortable with her. Plus they never argued, as he and his girlfriends often did. Sylvia did not demand much from him, just satisfying sexual encounters and the occasional dinner ordered in.

Once in a while, Eric would suggest that they go to a sex club, or a strip show. His girlfriend wouldn't go for that, but Sylvia didn't mind. In fact, she found those venues interesting and even educational. Although some of what she saw wasn't her cup of tea, she had no problem with going along just to see what happened there. Her open and nonjudgmental attitude was exactly what Eric needed to allow himself to satisfy his own curiosity about sex.

When Eric started that second job as a real estate broker, his time became more precious. He was living with his girlfriend. Yet he still saw Sylvia at least once or twice a week, even while working two jobs. The old saying, "Where there's a will, there's a way," certainly held true in Eric's case. He made the time to meet with Sylvia even though a casual observer (and Eric's girlfriend) would have said the man had no time for an affair.

Most men *will* make the time for sex, whether it's with their wives or the other woman. (See the next chapter for what they may be looking for.) If you think your husband or boyfriend doesn't have time for an affair, better adjust your thinking. He will let go of something else in his schedule (a client meeting, a haircut, time at the gym) to make room for sex. He'll take a few hours off for a non-existent doctor's appointment if that's what's required. But few men will miss an opportunity for sex.

Sylvia noticed that although Eric still went on vacations from time to time with his girlfriend, he would always see Sylvia they day before he left and the day he returned. He would let Sylvia know the dates in advance and asked her to please find time for him.

Although it may seem that Sylvia was getting the short end of the stick (no pun intended), since she was not the woman going on these vacations, Sylvia didn't mind. She had her own friends who vacationed together, and she really wouldn't have chosen the same vacation spots that Eric preferred. But think of how demoralizing it would have been for his girlfriend to know that her guy was seeing another woman right before they left and as soon as they returned from their holiday together.

Of course, Eric's girlfriend never found out, but was her ignorance really bliss? Put yourself in that girlfriend's shoes. Would you be okay with this situation just because you didn't know about it? Hardly. And yet, your man may be doing the same thing. Kind of takes the shine off that trip to Barbados, doesn't it?

Take it one step further. How often have you heard separate vacations touted in the media as a cure for the marital doldrums? "Absence makes the heart grow fonder," the age-old saying insists. But Sylvia can tell you, quite frankly, that you can't trust your boyfriend on a vacation away from you. In fact, you can't trust him if you're sleeping and he's awake.

Sylvia was also involved, at a later time, with Dean, a manufacturer's representative who traveled a lot. They met on an internet dating site, but soon they were meeting in person. Dean had appointments in Sylvia's city about once every month. During those visits, they would see films, go out to dinner, have long into-the-night conversations about philosophy and life, and, of course, great sex. Dean met other women in other cities, and Sylvia knew that. She was content to have one or two evenings a month with Dean that were totally enjoyable and free of commitment or responsibility. Sylvia never felt used. Dean spent plenty of money on their "dates" and really concentrated on being an entertaining partner. She, of course, reciprocated in her own special way. They were doing each other a favor by getting together, and maybe that made the other days of the month more tolerable for each.

Further Reading

Allen, Pat, and Don Schmincke (2009). *The Truth about Men Will Set You Free…but first it'll p*ss you off!* Newport Beach, CA: The WANT Institute.

Zinczenko, David (2006). *Men, Love & Sex.* NY: Rodale, Inc.

"It's a lot of fun to be able to sleep with somebody on a Monday night and sleep with someone different on a Tuesday night, and I felt no guilt about it at all."

~ David Wygant (2011) in "Multiple Sex Partners." AskMen.com.

Straight from the Cougar's Mouth:

"My younger guy wants sex every which way. Granted, some of his ideas come from porn. But he's tired of hearing 'No!' at home when he tries something new. He's tired of boring sex."

> *"In this new century, sex and relationships are rapidly changing. We are poised to enter an entirely new realm of sexuality, where old taboos are busted, and more and more people are open to bold, expansive ideas about sex."*
>
> ~ Tristan Taormino, *Down and Dirty Sex Secrets*

6 • Circus sex??

(Caution: You may not want to know.)

Anne's Story

It's been a few years since Anne was the pitiable wife being cheated upon. Maybe fifteen. But those memories die hard, as painful and unexpected as they were. She can still remember the afternoon she found out that her husband, the father of their three children, was cheating on her.

Jack had left early that morning on a business trip to Montreal, and somehow in all the frantic activity of a typical morning, walking the dog and getting the kids off to school, Anne suddenly realized that she had neglected to get the phone number or even the name of the hotel at which he was staying. (This was in the days before cell phones.) So after dropping the kids off, she returned home and called his office. Surely someone there could give her that information. She asked to speak to Tom, his boss.

Imagine her surprise when, at first, Tom hesitated, then said in a quieter voice, "Anne, Jack's not on a business trip. He's just taken a few days off. I have no idea how to get in touch with him." Anne felt like someone had landed a one-two punch to her abdomen. Evidently her husband had lied to her. And suddenly all the odd, inexplicable phone calls of the past several weeks added up quite neatly: He was having an affair!

After the initial shock wore off, and after she pulled herself back together, Anne consulted a clinical psychologist with whom she'd once done an internship. She thought perhaps he could shed some light on why this husband and father would risk losing his family over some other woman.

What the good doctor revealed, and what she subsequently discovered on her own, years later, in the role of "the other woman" herself, would make her wish her mother had been a little more explicit in her advice to Annie, the young bride. She has tried to communicate much of her hard-earned wisdom to her twenty-something daughter, alas to little or no avail. Perhaps the young female mind just won't accept these truths, or maybe they're just too, too unpleasant to contemplate. But Anne wants *you* to know:

Sex is far more important to most men than it is to the average woman. Immeasurably so. It's a drive, and it demands to be satisfied, if not by the wife, then by whoever else steps up to the plate. On some level, women know that, but once settled into marriage, we prefer to think that our husbands are more similar to us than dissimilar. It's simply not true. Males are referred to as the *opposite sex* for a reason. They generally want more sex, more variety, and kinkier sex than would make most women happy. (Of course, there are exceptions to every rule, but unless you're absolutely certain you're married to him, you'd better keep on reading.)

As has been mentioned before, men also use sex to measure their mettle as men. If they are not having plenty of it, with lots of variety, and maybe several partners, they just don't measure up in their own eyes or in the eyes of their buddies.

The woman he chooses for an affair is available and willing. She has no children or is able to get away from them on short notice. She is always ready to receive him sexually in the manner he prefers. Anal sex? You got it. Plenty of oral? You bet. Maybe a strap-on or a harness and a couple of vibrating bullets? Bring it on! Even threesomes or partner swapping may be on the menu if your man has been experimenting for quite some time. He probably does not want to lose you and the children, but he knows there's something missing (sexually) from the marriage, and he has figured out where to get it.

Sex with the other woman helps him achieve the frequency he desires. He may not even be getting mind-blowing sex from her. He may just need more of the regular vanilla stuff than you currently provide. Perhaps your magic number is three times a week, his is seven, or nine, or twelve. Get the picture? She is picking up your slack. Think back to how often you had sex when you were just going together, not married. He still wants it that often, but if you've had children, or put on weight, care for an aging parent, or spend more hours at work now than before, chances are you don't want sex as often as he does.

Twelve times a week *does* seem a bit excessive to most women. But sex is one requirement that really cannot be negotiated. Think about other commitments you have made: the plants need to be watered according to their individual needs or they die; the dog needs to be walked four times a day or you're going to clean up his messes; your Mom needs a phone call from you once a day or she'll be calling the local hospitals and the police. If you have hooked up with a man who needs sex twelve times a week, *he needs sex twelve times a week.* From you or *somebody*! It's a non-negotiable. End of discussion.

Sex with the older woman gives him the experiences you no longer want to share with him. Remember how you used to do it? Doggy-style in front of a window, in a tent in the backyard, in goofy motels with mirrors on the ceilings and porn channels on the tv? When's the last time you indulged in that kind of play? Not since the kids came along, most probably. Well, guess what? He misses the playfulness of those times. In survey after survey, men respond that one quality they desire in a partner is *playfulness* (not affection, which is what most women would respond). When that playfulness is gone from your marriage, so is your man. Elvis has left the building.

Circus Sex: He can do things with the other woman he'd be embarrassed to do with you (if you'd even *let* him!). Think of a fetish you'd rather not accommodate. (Come on, you've read *Savage Love.*) Your infantilized man in diapers, coming to Mama for suckling and cuddling. Your submissive man with a Canadian prison strap or bullwhip in his hand, needing discipline. Your cross-dressing man in your red satin chemise. Golden showers. Strap-on dildos. Idiosyncratic costumes. Bondage. Lap dances. Stripteases. Swapping urine cocktails. Whatever his kinky desires, you've probably made it clear by now that you're not interested in *those* kinds of adventures. He will not ask you again. If you make him feel embarrassed about his wants, he'll find another woman who isn't so judgmental and who will indulge him. Yes, she'll lick his ass.

Men today have seen images in porn that their fathers never did. They want some of those images realized in their bedrooms and with their wives or girlfriends. Do you have the *right* to refuse to let him cum on your face and breasts? Or to pee in your mouth? Of course you do. But remember: if he wants it, he'll get it from someone else.

He still loves the variety that different bodies offer, and he can't give it up. Remember what a "catch" he was when you first met him? He may not have been a player, exactly, but no doubt he was linked to several different women before you came into the picture. Maybe you even got him to open up about the women he knew before you. You were flattered that out of all the woman he *could* have had, he selected you.

The only problem is that he misses that variety now. He still wants a different woman now and then, just to add a little spice to his sex life. (Read some of the copy in men's online dating profiles. See how often the word "spice" shows up – almost as often as the word "fun.") He may not have a harem mentality exactly, but he definitely gets off on the notion of having more than one woman. Blonde, brunette, redhead. Different races and ethnic groups. Different body types. Sometimes all in the same day.

Men's brains are wired to respond to a female body, even if it's not a *Playboy* body. The curves that adorn a pleasingly plump marketing assistant are just as womanly as the tighter, gym-toned body of the personal trainer. They're just two ways of being female. And female is what attracts most men. In fact, the very differences between two women make them both desirable.

For some men, different personalities make it exciting. The other woman may be the direct opposite of who you are. While you consider yourself a world class homemaker and nurturer, she may be a budding entrepreneur, focused on building her fledgling business. You may be all high maintenance and Gucci, while she is plain folk and happy with a much simpler life. Maybe you and your man can discuss stock portfolios like a couple of crazed investment bankers, but she plays jazz piano and still sings professionally on occasion.

Men often want it all and find it difficult, if not impossible, to give any of it up. They just can't visualize spending the rest of their lives (and all their intimate times) with only one woman. So he goes to see her at the club where she's performing, or he installs new accounting software on her computer. And all the while you think he's working late or stopping by his buddy's place for a quick beer, because that's what he told you. (Oh, did we forget to mention that he *will lie* when it serves his purposes?)

Think about the fantasies he may still savor. Has he ever had two women at the same time (MFF) or two women, separately, in the same day? Is there a sex club that he's mentioned, or has he asked you to go there with him? Has he always been a breast man, and yours are a tad smallish? Does he dream of women from exotic places or different cultures? What kinds of porn does he enjoy? Alexis Texas's ass? Girl-on-girl? His fantasies may be more than just fond memories from his bachelorhood. By now, they may be an integral part of who he is as a person.

Fantasies can be nothing more than mental amusements that fill a man's head when he just wants to relax. Or they can be the motivations which lead him to the other woman. Every wife or girlfriend should know what fantasies her man harbors in his heart. If she can't or won't help him to enjoy them, to realize them, in some way with her, then he's ripe for the other woman.

Both Nina and Anne have had breast enlargements. Nina had always been small, and Anne's breasts shrunk markedly during her childbearing and breastfeeding years. Some people would criticize them for having surgically altered their bodies to appeal to men, but both women agree that it was the right thing to do. Their men love their bigger breasts, and that suits Nina and Anne just fine.

Candice and Jerry were lovers for about three years. He and his wife Bea had met at church (that's good, right?), dated, and married. Spiritually and intellectually they were a perfect match. They agreed on almost every major issue that couples face. But after marriage, Jerry found that Bea would not or could not do certain things that he desperately wanted to experience. She wouldn't have sex anywhere but in their bed. She wouldn't let him fondle her in semi-public places, like the car or the movie theater. She wouldn't try anal sex. And she would give him only perfunctory oral sex. What led Jerry to Candice was not a loss of love for his wife. He continued to love her and make love to her, as much as she would allow. But his fantasies drove him also into Candice's arms. Jerry's experience is shared by many.

Of course, some men discover (or finally admit) they're bi-curious after marrying. They may wish to explore that side of their sexuality without provoking you "unnecessarily." In that case, you'd be wondering, about now, what does he do with *him?* And what can you do about that? But, unfortunately, that's a whole other book.

Men have learned it's a good idea to cultivate a spare. Of course, this attitude reeks of objectifying women, but for most men it's the way they feel. If they need sex, the same way they sometimes need a cold beer or a pizza, they have to develop a source. If you and he are arguing, he can always spend the night at the cougar's place. (He'll tell you he's at his buddy's apartment.) Even if he comes home to you at night, he may take the afternoon off from work (without letting you know) and spend it in bed with her. Once he has you comfortably in a routine, he learns to say and do the things that reassure you he's a faithful guy, and then he can do pretty much whatever he wants.

Anne says, "When my ex was cheating, I didn't have a clue. I was soooo sure he was faithful to me! He always acted like a faithful man. Even brought me flowers for no apparent reason."

For men, sex is often more of a sport than a romantic encounter. Just as in sports, they

crave excitement with their sex. "In carrying out my roles as the other woman, I've had requests for domination, for submission, for dirty talk, for spankings (both giving and receiving), for golden showers (both giving and receiving), for costumes (nurse, schoolgirl, business attire, police officer, showgirl, etc.), and for every kind of sex act imaginable, with or without the accompaniment of toys. I once gave a guy carte blanche over a week-long holiday to have sex as often as he wanted, and I think now I know what a hooker must feel like when the convention is in town. I was convinced I was making up for twelve years of his wife's disinterest in sex.

"I've met men in motels who had to bring their dogs or babies with them. I've sat on men's faces and let them suck my ass. I've gone to men's homes to administer blowjobs while their wives were at work, sometimes in the marital bed. I've had sex with men on their desks at the office (not often), in the men's room (several times), and at their buddies' homes (only twice). A favorite among some men is sex in a department store dressing room. (That one can be difficult to pull off.) I've done a police officer in his squad car while he was on duty. I know a female teacher who had sex with a male teacher at the school in an equipment closet. The possibility of discovery is apparently a potent aphrodisiac for many men.

"Despite what you may want to believe, Brett Favre wasn't the first man to forward a photo of his equipment to a woman. Almost all of my partners have texted me photos of their hard cocks at one time or another. It's a fishing expedition for compliments, I know, which I am happy to indulge. While with me, men have sniffed or swallowed substances designed to enhance their orgasms. I've given lap dances and received them. I've used sex swings, spanking tables, and other sex furniture that men's wives would be squeamish about trying. In restaurants, I've been fingered, felt up, and even partly fisted. I've had my arms and legs bound or strapped to a bed, or been strung up on Shibari ropes and done my share of tying men up as well. I've spent more money on five-inch heels and fishnet stockings than I care to remember. I've masqueraded as a real estate buyer and met men in vacant condominiums for sex on the plush new carpeting. One fellow just wanted me to wear clothing that gave him instant access to my body all day at work. Another loved for me to strip to music for him. Whatever may be different from the sex you and your husband have at home, qualitatively or quantitatively, that's what he gets from me.

"Perhaps the greatest surprises I've discovered are that men will risk losing their entire families to fulfill their sexual needs, they will risk their jobs by using job-related venues for their sexual exploits, and they want all this extracurricular sex without condoms. What's that line about guys thinking with the little head? But many of these men are married and nevertheless deprived. One guy told me no woman had *ever* licked his balls before. Why would a woman marry a guy and then refuse to do what makes him happy?"

Actually we have seen plenty of people in public office or highly visible occupations who have risked their marriages and family life for some risky sex. Doesn't that tell you how important the right kind of sex is to a man?

An erotic massage while viewing porn may be just what your man needs after a hard day at work. The cougar will give him the attention he needs without complaining that she doesn't have the time or that she just gave him a massage Tuesday. She doesn't mind watching porn, either, which you may have decided has no place in your life now that you have kids. Today's man has grown up with porn and won't give it up.

Many women accommodate their men quite well sexually before marriage (or before moving in together), and then decide that there are some things they're not going to do any more once the relationship seems permanent. Maybe it's dressing up in stockings and heels for him. Maybe it's a particular sex act, like swallowing his cum. Or maybe it's the backrubs and massages that brought them close in the first place. For men, that's tantamount to bait-and-switch at the department store. They feel they've been lured into a relationship with a woman by the promise of certain behaviors, and then, when they make a commitment, those behaviors suddenly disappear.

Think about your own relationship with your guy. What's he missing that you used to provide so willingly? Maybe the cougar is providing it these days. Maybe she's sitting on his face.

Sometimes they just talk. Yes, really. That's not the most common reason men take up with cougars, but it does make the list.

A cougar may be better educated than you, or just more adept at sparkling conversation. She may simply have a more upbeat personality. She may have had experiences that you have not, and your man can talk to her about them.

The woman your man is seeing will avoid arguing with him. She may be skilled at getting him to open up and vent his feelings, or she may simply provide a safe environment in which he can talk freely without fear that something he says will be thrown back in his face at some future time. She compliments him freely. Remember that the relationship between your man and his older woman doesn't carry the burdens of making a life together or raising a family. When they get together, it's just him and her. We agree it's not fair. It just is what it is.

Have you ever listened to how women talk to their husbands? Try it sometime, when you're at WalMart or Home Depot. Has that whiny, demanding tone crept into your voice over the years? Do you sound more like his mother than his lover? Take that as a cue that something has eroded in your relationship if you no longer speak to him the dulcet tones of the past.

So what can you do if you suspect your husband is straying? Well, first of all the two of you obviously need to talk, calmly, about what's happening. Chances are good he's not in love with the other woman, but he *is* getting something from her that he needs. Are you willing to provide those experiences for him? Can you be both the madonna and the whore in his life? Would you be willing to try? Does he want to save his marriage? Do you? Can he refrain from going outside the marriage if you deliver more of what he needs at home?

Of course, a trained couples therapist may be able to ascertain the likelihood of you two being able to work things out satisfactorily. Doing so may require some serious adjustments on your part and on your spouse's, but remember what was said earlier: *On some level, women know that males and females are opposites, yet once settled into marriage, we prefer to see our husbands as more similar to us than dissimilar.* Any other man you might trade him for is likely to come with that same feature. Assuming you still love him, doesn't it make sense to work with the man you already have?

Further Reading

Pierce Buxton, Amity (1994). *The Other Side of the Closet: The Coming-Out Crisis for Straight Spouses and Families.* NY:John Wiley & Sons.

Taormino, Tristan (2001). *Down and Dirty Sex Secrets.* NY: HarperCollins Publishers Inc.

"Men – gay, straight, bi – tend to be sluts."

~ Dan Savage,
SavageLove (2011)

Straight from the Cougar's Mouth:

"I don't think I would ever get married again. Knowing what I know about men now, and how easy it is for them to get sex without being discovered, I could never trust a husband."

Ask Yourself:

- When was the last time you tried something new in bed?
- Do you sometimes feel like an old married couple already?
- What would he go looking for outside your relationship if he were to go looking?
- Can you provide that at home?

"Most women would probably agree that any man who cheats on his woman just because she puts on a few extra pounds never truly loved her in the first place. However, men do not love as unconditionally as women do. We are visual creatures who live in a society where a great deal of emphasis is put on physical appearance. In our minds, we expect the woman we love to remain beautiful, and thin, throughout eternity."

~ Michael Baisden, *Never Satisfied: How & Why Men Cheat*

7 • The High-Maintenance Man

Nina's Story

"I walked into the room and kind of caught him off-guard. He was sitting in front of the computer, and on the screen was this extremely hot woman, grinding her ass into a guy's face! I mean, his nose was right in her ass! I knew right then that I could never compete with that. Sometimes he watches he-shes doing it. He doesn't know that I know. But it creeps me out to know. I just wonder what's going through his mind."

~ A woman Nina works with

Does your guy watch porn? A little? Or a lot? Do you catch him shutting down his computer when you enter the room? Does he sometimes need to work online after you've gone to bed? Do you know for a fact that spends time away from you or the family to view porn videos? You've got yourself a high-maintenance man.

Did your boyfriend have a lot of women before you? Did you discover that he and some buddies visited prostitutes or hired escorts in his previous life? Do his eyes wander toward beautiful women when you're out for dinner? Then you've got yourself a high-maintenance man.

Was your sex life with him much hotter before the kids came along? Did you do things sexually back then that you no longer do? Does he sometimes mention that you're not as wild as you used to be? Does he want sex all the time? Well, then, sister, you've got yourself a high-maintenance man.

If he is attractive to other women, you can be sure that he knows it. Particularly at work, where women might not know his relationship status, women will come on to him. And if he's resisted them up till now, it's only because he's been trying to be the kind of man you want him to be.

But are you still the kind of woman he wants you to be? Many women alter their behavior after they have "caught" the man of their dreams. What they fail to realize is that by being in a relationship with you, he has had to swear off intimate contact with other women. He's put all his eggs into one basket, so to speak – you. And if you suddenly change the behavior that attracted him to you in the first place, he's going to feel that all deals are off. Maybe not today. Maybe not tomorrow. But eventually.

We women think it's unfair that men dump their girlfriends or wives when they put on a few pounds. After all, we don't get outraged if our men put on a little weight. In fact, we often think it's cute – it means he's happy and content. But here is one of those situations where men and women are so different. A wise old observation says:

A man marries a woman for who she is today. A woman marries a man for who she thinks he can be tomorrow.

So keep that wedding photograph nearby and compare yourself to it. Your man is comparing you to it every day.

You probably have a girlfriend who married her boyfriend, helped put him through college or grad school, then helped him establish his business or professional practice, all the while sacrificing some of her own goals for what she wanted him to be. Yet we seldom hear of a man who married a girl who was overweight and undereducated, enrolled her in Weight Watchers and sacrificed his own career to help her earn a degree and make something of herself. (Well, there is that one old story, Pygmalion, but frankly that about exhausts the topic.) Women, largely being nurturers, put themselves second and care for the needs of their husbands and children. But men tend to put *themselves* first, and so they marry the woman that fits their needs best at that moment in time. They marry the best-looking, best-educated, sexiest woman they think they can get. He picked you. Flattering, right?

But that's where the trouble lies. You have a tall order to live up to. In his eyes, when you begin to fall short of that ideal that he thought you matched when he first dated you, he feels cheated. You must constantly try to be that girl he married, even as the years roll by, as children come into the picture, as your circumstances wax and wane.

Now add to those requirements the new requirements that our culture is expecting of women. All men have viewed at least some porn. Some men view more than others, some are addicted to a dysfunctional degree. Wherever your man stands on the porn continuum, he will constantly measure you against what he sees on his monitor. Unless he married you for your money, chances are very good that he married you for the sexual being that thought you were (because that's what you led him to believe). Oh, sure, he wanted an intelligent woman, someone he could bring home to his parents, someone who could raise his children to be self-sufficient, honorable members of society.

But do you think he was visualizing his future children when you and he first began having a sexual relationship? Hell no. He was thinking about himself, and his satisfaction. He was secretly smiling to himself about the "hot" woman he had snared. He looked forward to those bedroom, auto, pool-table, motel sessions the same way a hungry man looks forward to his next meal. Trust this: there wasn't any thought of future children on his mind back then.

So after deciding to become exclusive, maybe move in together, maybe even marry, he really didn't expect things to change. Yet we all know that women's biological clocks often put pressure on them to start planning the next stage of the relationship: the childbearing stage. Or at the very least, if the pressure to have children is not yet present, the comfort of knowing that she has her man often makes a woman less focused on the features that attracted him in the first place.

There are several common complaints that men will express to their cougars (when they finally decide to get one):

"She just sort of let herself go after we moved in together."

"She takes me for granted now. She used to be excited to see me, but now she greets me at the door with a list of issues I need to attend to, if she greets me at all."

"Once the kids came along, they took first place in her mind. I became the bill-payer, or the one who helps her raise the kids. I'm not number one any more."

"We hardly ever have sex these days. And when we do, it's not like it used to be. It's frankly boring."

Think about those comments. Can you imagine any of them coming out of your guy's mouth? All it takes is one to steer his imagination toward the cougar. Let two of them fall from his lips and you can just about bet the farm on it. The cougar promises to give him whatever it is he needs without making him give up what he has at home. Cake and eat it!

The truth is that a man will not usually *leave* his girlfriend or wife for the cougar. He has too much to lose if he's married, and he often feels he can't bring his cougar around to his parents or friends because of the difference in their ages. This kind of May-December relationship, while becoming more acceptable in the U.S. today, is still not the norm. So what wives and girlfriends are discovering, more and more, is that their men are satisfying some of their needs in the primary relationship and other needs in the cougar relationship. It appears that it takes more than one woman to satisfy some men.

To the men involved, it only seems fair. If their wives or girlfriends are not living up to the reality they seemed to have promised back when they first met, then the guys will simply find their missing satisfactions covertly elsewhere. Most women would not knowingly agree to this plan. They would say (and you probably would, too) that they didn't sign up for that. Of course, the men would counter that *they* aren't getting what *they* signed up for either, and that's why they turned to the other woman.

Nina found, to her surprise, that she too couldn't seem to satisfy all her needs with one man. After her divorce, she met many men from several places: work, internet dating sites, a church group for divorced Catholics. Many of the men had some sort of tragic flaw that had propelled them toward divorce. Some had addiction problems (alcohol or gambling). Some were continually in financial trouble. Others seemed like children in men's clothing, never having matured emotionally, always looking for the next "good time." But there were, of course, decent men in the bunch. What Nina found was that one man didn't satisfy all her needs. She had denied some of her cravings in her marriage because she had wanted to be the good wife. But now that she was unattached, she didn't see the necessity for "settling" for less than she wanted out of life.

And so for Nina, and others like her, it takes a few good men to make her happy. Thus, she is friendly with a couple of older men with whom she socializes and occasionally travels. And she always has a younger man or two who provide the sexual fireworks that make her feel alive and young again. She understands the need for variety.

Where did she meet her first younger man? At the school where they both work. Did she pursue him? Not at all. He made the first (and the second, and the third) move. Nina knows there's no permanence in this relationship. But she's happy to have what she has for as long as it lasts. She doesn't pressure her guy to commit any further. She believes that pressuring a man, even though it may seem justified, will backfire. If men have one fatal flaw, it's an inability to deal with controlling women. So "laid back" is the name of the game.

Nina says, "Don't pressure him. Never demand. Ask in a nice way. Marriage (and a false sense of security) make women bitches. You don't need to drive your husband away by constantly nagging. Just hire somebody to paint the front porch if he won't do it, for crying out loud."

If women don't have all their needs met by one man, it shouldn't come as a surprise that men don't have all their needs met by one woman. Talk about it. That conversation should happen periodically, like a tune-up on a car. The small adjustments that might be necessary to keep you both happy are worth whatever effort it requires.

The high-maintenance man (like the high-maintenance woman) is a difficult partner to live with.

Your man may have convinced himself that he is more man than one woman can handle, and that spells trouble. If he thinks you can't provide all he needs to operate at his peak condition (and that includes not only sex, but verbal reinforcement, good household management, and whatever other requirements he has established), then he will feel within his rights to look outside your relationship for fulfillment. No, he's not a king, but know the consequences if you don't treat him like one.

Sometimes you can tell when something's up. Nina says her ex used to whistle a lot when he was having an affair. He felt so smug, so satisfied, that he would involuntarily whistle at home around Nina. Now Nina knows how to look for signs that a man is getting his needs met elsewhere, but involuntary smiles, sounds, and behaviors that are not part of a man's normal repertoire are a good place to begin looking. Smoothing his hair in a mirror (if he doesn't normally do that), getting a daydreamy look when he's just staring out the window, almost any evidence of "newfound happiness" can be a giveaway that a man has entered into a part-time parallel universe with someone else.

Nina knows her husband really believed he deserved an extra woman or two. He told her so after they divorced! She says his exact words were, "Some guys are just too much man for one woman."

Now *that* was a high-maintenance man.

Further Reading

Baisden, Michael (1995); *Never Satisfied: How & Why Men Cheat*. Atlanta:Legacy Publishing.

Easton, Dossie & Janet W. Hardy (2009). *The Ethical Slut: A Practical Guide to Polyamory, Open Relationships & Other Adventures.* Berkeley, CA: Celestial Arts.

"The cruelest lies are often told in silence."

~ Robert Louis Stevenson

"Look as hot as you can, and carry yourself with an inner monologue of 'I'm hot, and I don't give a fuck.' You'd be surprised at how attractive that is to men."

~ Steve Santagati in *The Manual: A True Bad Boy Explains How Men Think, Date, and Mate – and What Women Can Do to Come Out on Top*

8 • Sins of Omission

Sheila's Story

Do men lie more easily than women? Well, that depends on the man or woman in question, of course. But as a general rule, yes, men find it easier to lie. They often lie at work to cover themselves, or to appear more competent than they really are. They lie about their bowling scores or how many beers they can down and still remain standing. It's not hard then to carry over successful lying to the home front when a man believes it is necessary.

Our cougars have found that their young men lie, too. Not only to their girlfriends or wives but to the cougars as well. Smith and Doe, in their now-classic text, *What Men Don't Want Women to Know: The Secrets, the Lies, the Unspoken*

Truth, joke that "It's not a lie if you tell it to a woman." That statement may make a man laugh out loud, but, to a woman, it's a sad piece of reality that she must begin to deal with. Perhaps more insidious than outright lying, however, is men's tendency to omit the truth: what is often called the sin of omission.

You've done it yourself. Think back to when you were in high school and one of your parents was giving you the third degree about some date or dance. Your dad might have asked, "So did they serve alcohol at this party?" and you quickly replied, "Of course not! Jennifer's mom was there!" knowing that although the hosts did not *serve* alcohol, plenty of guests brought their own and drank it secretly, in the bathroom or in their cars.

Or on a more serious note, if you had an abortion in your teens, you may not tell your spouse about it. It only becomes a problem if he asks you outright if you've ever had one. Then, you will have to decide to come clean or lie.

Your boyfriend or husband uses the same technique of omission in responding to your questions (if he's not outright lying, of course). For instance, if he's going out of town on a business trip, you might ask, "Are any of the women from the office going on this trip?" His answer might be, "No, it's just the four of us guys, the account execs." And that answer satisfies you. What he doesn't tell you is that those four guys have every intention of visiting some strip clubs after the workday is done, or maybe even connecting with an escort service. Because *you didn't ask the right question*, you got only some of the information you really wanted. Your guy didn't exactly lie; he just neglected to tell you the whole truth.

Another favorite ploy of men is to make the woman feel ashamed that she even asked the question. Sheila remembers asking her young man if he had found another woman because he hadn't called her in a week. He replied, with a sneer, "Oh, sure, you know me. I'm out in the alley, out in the parking lot, back in the stockroom with some babe all the time." Men may use verbal irony to make *you* feel ashamed that you doubted their sincerity. You need to know your man.

Sheila's younger man would meet her after work for a quick dinner, conversation and of course some sex, but then he'd hurry back to the office to finish up some paperwork than needed to be done for a client. If his girlfriend asked him where he'd been so long, he could truthfully respond that he had some documents to send out that took longer than he expected. He would certainly not mention the meeting with Sheila. Again, the sin of omission accomplishes his end.

This practice is deadly, because it becomes habitual, just as lying can become habitual. The more one does it, the easier it gets. What the sin of omission requires of a girlfriend or wife is that she phrase her questions in such a way that her man cannot weasel out of an answer without either telling her the truth or lying. For example, instead of asking, "Are any of the women from the office going on this trip?" a woman should ask, "Are you guys expecting to have any sexual contact with women while you're on this trip?" It's pretty hard for a man to answer a question like that without either lying or tipping his hand. But it also makes the woman asking the question seem like a suspicious bitch.

Sometimes a man will volunteer information that you didn't even ask for. That's a red flag as well. When he says, "Jim and Ted and I went to this cool theme restaurant when we were in Atlanta where the whole place was decked out like a ship. The seafood was fantastic!" By mentioning the names of two coworkers, he implies that only the three of them went out to eat. But the part he omits is that each of them brought along their (female) administrative assistants. Or whoever those stunning women were.

A guy who's been divorced and now dating you may say he spent the weekend with his son and daughter. He'll say they went to Six Flags and had a great time. What he omits telling you is the minor detail that his ex-wife also went along, and she had a great time too. You have to know what questions to ask, even when a man seems to be giving you information willingly.

A word of caution: Although a woman's careful phrasing of questions can sometimes ferret out the truth, more often than not it simply pushes the guy over the line. Since he no longer can rely on omission to keep his secrets, he is forced into outright lying. Which is worse? Lying or partial truth? They are both deadly to your relationship.

The sin of omission is a difficult problem to deal with, just as lying is. Once again, a woman who suspects something is amiss needs to do some detective work on her own to find out what's going on. Sometimes being friendly with the girlfriends or wives of your man's friends and business associates is enough. Often the women will share what they know with one another and discrepancies will be discovered. But that doesn't always occur. Most of what you need to know you will have to ferret out on your own.

A woman should become familiar with body language signals that indicate a man might be lying or dodging the truth. Unless your guy is extremely well-practiced in the art of prevarication, he's likely to give off some of these cues when he's trying to avoid telling you the whole truth. It's a good idea to check out information on internet websites that focus on lying and body language so that you will not be clueless. Some of the most important signs that your man may be lying or omitting the whole truth are:

- Avoiding eye contact with you

- Difficulty speaking, or speaking in an unusual fashion, unlike his ordinary speech
- Pausing to plan his answer before speaking
- Becoming stiff or physically uncomfortable
- Getting agitated or redirecting the blame onto you for being suspicious
- Leaving the room or angrily refusing to discuss the issue at all

Along with the sin of omission, many men practice a sort of "sexual free-pass system" in which they believe they can permit themselves to have sexual or other intimate relationships so long as they impose certain limits that supposedly "honor" the marriage contract. For example, some men will not kiss the cougar (or a prostitute) on the lips. That behavior is reserved for the wife alone. Who made up that rule? He did! Probably because he's not that much into kissing anyway, and he knows it's his wife's favorite intimacy.

Other men will not cum inside the cougar's body. They always pull out and finish off manually. That reserves the most intimate part of the sex act for the wife. Some men won't cuddle with the other woman. Some won't spend the whole night. Some insist on using a motel. Every man is different, but most devise these "charms" or "magical conditions" that, to their minds anyway, make the relationship with the cougar acceptable. Acceptable to whom? Probably NOT to the wife or girlfriend who has no idea of what's going on.

How does this "free pass system" begin? It may begin with the couple themselves. The wife or girlfriend may have said, at some point, "I would just die if I found out you kissed another woman. Promise you won't ever do that to me." Or she may have indicated that certain behaviors are very important to her and must be reserved for her. "I hope you never spent the night spooning with anyone before me. I like to think of that as our special thing." That comment suggests to her man that spending the night spooning would be a no-no. A man listens for these free passes whenever you speak. What they do is satisfy your man that, no matter what else he *is* doing, he is not doing the *one thing* that would hurt you the most if you knew. And isn't that admirable of him?

One of Candice's young men used to go on an annual extended weekend golf outing to North Carolina with several of his friends. It really was a guys-only trip, and apparently they all stayed together in a rented house and there was no hanky-panky going on, just golf. But he would call Candice, late at night, for phone sex before he went to sleep. Now, he could have called his wife, but Candice assumes that his wife was no longer interested in phone sex, if she ever was. Even if this young man's wife asked him pointedly if he had sex with any woman while he was in North Carolina, he would probably answer "no" and feel that he was being honest. But put yourself in his wife's place: if she knew about the phone sex, would she consider that cheating? Maybe she would.

Dan Crum, a former CIA polygraph investigator and expert interrogator has written one of the most useful books a woman could possibly read. *Is He Lying to You?* not only explains how to go about framing questions to bring out the many deceitful ploys your man may be using to keep you clueless and ignorant of his behavior, but it also helps you identify truthfulness traits in men's conversation. Plus, the author's explanation of how body language can reveal the deceiver's lying behavior is worth the price of the book. With a little practice, women can become more proficient at sniffing out liars and con artists.

Just remember not to tip your hand by telling your guy what you're up to. Don't explain how you know that he's lying – that will only make him more cautious in the future. Just use the information you gather to help you assess your relationship. By sharing with him what you've learned to look for, you just make his deceit easier to accomplish. Remember, he doesn't share everything with you.

All of this cheating, lying, prevaricating, and misleading stems from a basic difference between men and women: Men, for the most part, do not see sex as a sacred bond between two people. For most men, sex is just that inelastic demand, like hunger, thirst, or fatigue, that needs to be addressed on a regular basis. And so to address it, they sometimes feel they must devise elaborate mental constructs to enable them to get what they need whether inside or outside the relationship. Women call it "having your cake and eating it, too." Men don't see it that way.

Sheila once asked her guy if he didn't think his wife would be terribly hurt if she found out about them. But he assured her, "You know, I don't love my wife any less because I have sex with you." And he probably meant it. The trouble is nobody consulted his wife to see if *she* would love *him* any less for having sex with someone other than her.

Further Reading

Crum, Dan (2010). *Is He Lying to You?* Franklin Lakes, NJ: Career Press.

Santagati, Steve (2007). *The Manual: A True Bad Boy Explains How Men Think, Date, and Mate – and What Women Can Do to Come Out on Top.* NY:Three Rivers Press.

"Sure enough, we only had a short-term fling. Eventually things got boring and we became too busy for each other. But she taught me something. Either that or she corrupted me. In my opinion nothing changed at home. What I did with her had no effect at home. I can say that truthful and with a straight face. All the fun I have outside of my marriage since then hasn't had any effect either.

"In my mind I think it even helps my relationship with my wife. (I know most people would totally shake their head in disbelief.) Here is why I say that. I love my wife. I don't want to leave her. I love my kids. I don't want to leave them. But I am also not 100% satisfied at home. Life is short and you only get one shot. I don't like sitting around bored, looking forward to super-boring sex with my wife time and time again.

"Yet when I go outside my marriage and get to bang a woman that is horny and looking for the same thing I am....Well, that is awesome."

~ From a cheater's blog

Straight from the Cougar's Mouth:

"Sometimes he calls you when you're working or at your parents' house. You think it's sweet that he misses you, but he's really just calling to make sure you are where you said you'd be, so that we can hook up."

"I think men are deeply attracted to a woman who knows what it's all about and is sexually free," said Pepper Schwartz, a sociologist at the University of Washington and a sex columnist and author. "The idea of a woman who is sexually knowledgeable and passionate is very attractive to a lot of young men who are getting more hesitant interactions or conditional sexual access from younger women."

> ~ Sarah Kershaw (10/14/2009), Rethinking the Older-Woman-Younger-Man Relationship," *New York Times*

9 • How Young? How Old?

Sylvia once asked 30-year-old Frank if he slept with other women on his many business trips to East Coast financial hubs. "You know, I don't," he answered. "When I'm out on business, I just don't have the time to wine 'em and dine 'em the way they want. So I usually just watch some porn, masturbate, and go to sleep." For Frank, as for most men, sex is a basic drive. He doesn't need for it to occur within a relationship.

You might guess that most of the men who would seek out a cougar are in their twenties or thirties. And you would be right. After all, we know men are horny as hell during those years. And, in addition, those are also the years of childbearing for girlfriends and wives, which tends to slow down the pace of sexual relations for a lot of couples. But just how young will a cougar venture?

A not-so-common cougar scenario involves the much younger and less experienced man – in his very early twenties. In earlier times, a father might have taken his son to an experienced woman in town, maybe a prostitute, who would introduce him to the mysteries of sex and its etiquette. Today, short of contacting an escort service himself, a young man would be more likely to try to find a "fast" girl to practice on. But some solicit the guidance and experience of an older woman known as a cougar.

After Anne's divorce, she joined a gym and began working on getting her figure back after three children. With a careful diet and four-day-a-week exercise program, it wasn't long before Anne had shed the post-pregnancy weight that had clung to her. Of course, with her husband gone, she now had to hire people to do some of the jobs he had done around the house. One of those jobs was lawn care. Anne hired a local high school senior, Nick, who seemed quite entrepreneurial and ambitious.

During several years of his yard work, Anne noticed that Nick was developing into quite a handsome, well-built young man. He went off to college, but made sure that Anne's lawn and yard were cared for in his absence by "underlings" from his neighborhood lawn care service whom he had trained. In the summers, when he was home, Nick did the work himself.

One Christmas break, Anne was at the gym running track, putting in her 30 minutes per day. Someone waved to her from the far side of the track. It was Nick. He was a senior in college now, home on break, and working out at the same gym.

They ran into each other a couple of times again at the gym, and finally, Nick asked Anne if he could speak to her about something kind of embarrassing. Anne said, "Of course."

Nick proposed that he and Anne become lovers. Not emotionally lovers, but physically lovers. He said he'd noticed how well she kept herself, and he had not really had a sex life since he started college, because classes and work consumed so much of his time. He dated occasionally, but not seriously, and he really felt it was time he learned about satisfying a woman. He knew Anne was alone and he found her attractive. Would she be interested?

Anne was floored. She had not seen this coming, and she wasn't sure how to handle it. Nick was a strong, masculine guy, but his family lived just a couple of blocks away, and she wondered could he be discreet? In fact, he was the one who brought up the need for discretion. He didn't want his mom or dad to know anything about this arrangement, if indeed Anne would go for it.

Anne gave it some thought. Nick was twenty-one, and he had obviously thought this over. He had even researched a motel that he thought they could use for their meetings. In the end, she said yes, and they began an almost year-long relationship that was unlike anything Anne had ever experienced in her rather unspectacular sex life. She taught Nick things about women's sexual response he might not learn for years, and of course he brought ideas to the table as well. His many midnight talks with his buddies at school and his familiarity with various kinds of porn made him an adventurous partner, and so both benefited from the relationship.

Cougars report that men whose wives are pregnant are highly likely to seek them out for sexual relations, if not for a more balanced relationship. The men find it frustrating that their wives' bodies have changed dramatically during pregnancy, sometimes making them unappealing, or at least awkward. First-time dads may also be afraid of hurting the developing fetus, and so they won't initiate sex as often, or at least not in the positions that they would like. Further, some women also become unreceptive to their partners' sexual advances during pregnancy for a variety of reasons. Sex may feel uncomfortable, they may have experienced a loss of libido, or they too fear hurting the baby. Most of all, the wife is totally focused on her pregnancy and not really interested in sex. For whatever reasons, pregnancy is *one of the critical times* in a woman's life when her partner is most likely to stray.

Once the children arrive, of course, life becomes a whirlwind of child-centered activity for most families. Women frequently tend to overdedicate their time to their children at the expense of their relationship with their spouse. That's understandable. They feel that their primary role is that of nurturer. But there's at least one person who's not feeling very nurtured at this point in time. The husband. More than one cougar has said her guy feels like "My wife doesn't know I exist anymore. It's all about the kids." A man whose wife is totally absorbed in motherhood will look for his carnal satisfactions outside the home. That is cougar territory.

Yet another dangerous time is the forties and fifties. Once a woman's childrearing is complete, she may view sex as no longer necessary. Her husband has become totally familiar to her, and the sexual excitement of early marriage is long past. Add to this the beginning of her menopausal period, and many men find their women at this stage of life uninterested in, if not downright repelled by, the idea of passionate sex. Many women say that their husbands have become more like brothers. It's more common than one would think for a woman of a certain age to tell her spouse, "I don't want to do this any more. We're too old." Generally the husbands disagree but are powerless to sway their unbending wives. The older man himself may then look for a cougar because he does not want to risk becoming a father again, which would be possibility with a younger partner, and because cougars have a reputation for being discreet and drama-free.

It appears that among men there is almost no age group that is immune to the appeal of the cougar. For whatever their reasons, men find themselves attracted to these women who offer what they can't get at home. And it isn't always just sex. When women are occupied with children, or their careers, or any other worthy cause, the person who feels left out of the picture is usually the man. Sure, sex plays a huge role in his sense of abandonment, since sex is one of the main ways a man feels connected to his partner. But often there are other emotional needs that are not being met as well.

Psychologists tell us that, while women need to feel affection, men need to feel appreciated. To maintain an adequate sense of self-worth, a man must believe that his partner truly appreciates the efforts he makes on behalf of her and/or the family. When that feeling of appreciation is missing, he may look for it elsewhere. Often, he does not even know what it is that he is looking for. He only knows it feels good when he finds it.

The cougar provides him with that feeling of being appreciated along with a healthy serving of sex. Your man may fix little things around her place, or share stock and investment tips, or just bring over some wine and pizza on one of his visits. The older woman makes sure he knows that his efforts were duly noted and complimented. And some men just liking having the older woman around as a confidence-booster that says they still have it goin' on.

Don't be alarmed, but your man often talks to the older woman about *you*, sometimes in an effort to understand behavior he finds perplexing, sometimes just to gripe and get things off his chest. To Nina, talking about the wife or girlfriend is perhaps one of the biggest betrayals a man can commit. It's such an invasion of your privacy. But there has usually been some breach in the relationship that pushes a man to ignore the typical boundaries we expect him to respect.

Nina says that the first time she and her young man got together, he was a stranger who surprised her by stopping by her house with his dog and baby son. He said he was attracted to her house and its interesting architectural features, but there was obviously more on his mind than just gables and clapboard siding. They didn't have sex that first time, of course. They just chatted over coffee about dogs, kids, and interesting houses. But the relationship had begun.

What men have that women generally don't is an amazing ability to compartmentalize different parts of their life. They can keep an affair, like one with a cougar, in one part of their head and never let it leak over into another part. It may not be a particularly admirable or ethical talent, but it does allow them to let "what happens in Vegas stay in Vegas." (That may work for a while, but we know that sooner or later what happens in Vegas *does* spill over into other areas of one's life.)

The cougar must learn to compartmentalize too, because her relationships with younger men are not societally sanctioned and cannot be discussed in conventional social circles without causing harm to someone. And except for a few couples like Demi and Ashton, most cougar relationships do not end up as long-term pairings. The cougar must learn to keep her emotions in check and her mouth shut.

It is for that reason, discretion, that the successful cougar is a woman who has learned to love sex for *sex*, not because it is an emotional experience or makes her feel closer to her guy. The really successful cougar compartmentalizes her recreational sex just like a man does. She accepts the relationship for what it is as well as for what it isn't. That takes practice, and it isn't easy, but apparently it can be done.

Further Reading

Gibson, Valerie (2008). *Cougar: A Guide for Older Women Dating Younger Men.* Toronto: Key Porter Books Ltd.

Matthews, David M. (2008). *Every Man Sees You Naked: An Insider's Guide to How Men Think.* Tucson:Wheatmark

Straight from the Cougar's Mouth:

"Now that he's got two kids, he says he's fucked. The carefree life he once visualized for himself will not be happening. So he believes that as long as he pays the bills he's entitled to whatever pleasures he can get it."

"Just looking for an older woman / cougar. Been obsessing over an older woman for some time. Am young , vibrant, and love to please. Help me fulfill this fantasy please!"

~ Male, 26, from craigslist.com

"Men feel important, special, and manly with the women with whom they have affairs. Their wives know every aspect of them and often let them know they're nothing special or, worse yet, a disappointment as a husband and a man."

~ Kara Oh , *Men Made Easy*

10 • Strategies to Find Out If He's Involved

Keep your eyes and ears open and your mouth shut. Like a detective, begin with the assumption that your quarry is guilty. Then find the evidence.

Candice's Story

There are always clues that a man is seeing another woman, but the wife or girlfriend, trusting soul that she is, doesn't notice them. She wants to believe her man is faithful to her.

When Candice was seeing a realtor, a man she met at work, she discovered how easy it was for him to find time for their meetings. He simply told his wife he had a property showing at whatever time was convenient for him and Candice. The wife knew that realtors were expected to be available 24/7, and so she never suspected anything. Candice and Greg would go to a distant Thai restaurant he liked (so he wouldn't run into anyone he knew) for a quiet dinner and then to a nearby motel for an hour or two.

Other men that Candice has been involved with similarly had jobs that made being away from home at odd hours seem normal. Teachers who coached after-school sports, dentists who had to see patients for emergencies, businessmen on business trips – all had legitimate reasons to be away from their wives at what most people would consider unusual hours. The wives had become conditioned to expect these strange hours, and the husbands' explanations seemed perfectly plausible.

But even keeping typical 9-5 work hours isn't necessarily a problem for the man who wants to have a cougar on the side.

The biggest problem for wives and girlfriends has been the invention of the cell phone. We are all so accustomed to using the cell phone for our personal calls that we miss the opportunity to call in through the company switchboard. Often the receptionist knows that your man has taken the afternoon off, but if you never speak to her, she can't tell you that he's out of the office.

And your man can use the cell phone to keep track of your activities. If he needs to know how you will be occupying the next three or four hours, all he has to do is call you on your cell and get your schedule. If you're working late or stopping at your mother's right after work, he knows he's bought some time.

When you call him on his cell, you don't know what you might be interrupting. Candice almost hates to admit it, but she's actually been giving a guy oral sex when his girlfriend called to confirm their plans for the rest of the evening. He signaled Candice not to stop! Think about that the next time you call your man on his cell.

So what is a girl to do? Well, for starters, just assume that your guy is cheating. That will put you in the right frame of mind to do what you have to do. (Of course, he may not be, but to find out, you'll have to make that assumption for now.) Follow some of these instructions to check on him and his word:

Become a sleuth. If he says he's bowling (or playing softball or watching a boxing match) with the guys, drive by and see if his car is actually parked nearby where it should be. Start calling him at work through the switchboard instead of his cell phone. If he's never there, that should be a red flag. If he tells you he's stopping by his sister's house, check with her later to see if he actually did. Look at the mileage on his odometer. Is he driving more than he usually does? Are gas station receipts from strange neighborhoods? Do these things discreetly, or you'll tip him off that you're on to him, and he'll start to be more cautious.

Check his Visa and Mastercard bills for unusual charges. One careless guy charged the motel room to his card and his wife woke him up in the middle of a Saturday afternoon nap to ask him about it. He denied that he had made the charge and ended up having to cancel the card when Visa refused to remove it, just so his wife would believe him. A hassle, just to cover his tracks, but the paper trail has always been problematic for men with infidelity on their minds. Look for charges for flowers, lingerie, and other gifts you know you didn't receive. Even paint! One guy bought paint for his cougar's entire apartment and charged it to his credit card.

Check his cell phone bill if you can. Look for high frequency numbers that you don't recognize and write them down. When you can, check his cell phone for those numbers. Chances are he's using a phony name for his cougar's number, but who else would he be calling at midnight? Even Tiger Woods's wife knew the cell phone held the answers she needed.

Start being more suspicious and vigilant about sex. You already know that new sex positions or interests can be a tip-off that he's learned something from another woman. Be aware if he suddenly wants anal sex or would like to try a little bondage if that's never been his style before. Similarly, if he's not much interested in sex at home any more, it may be because he's exhausted himself at the No-Tell Motel or his cougar's place. Scratches on his back or butt, a freshly-showered smell when he arrives home from a long day at work, even new underwear can mean trouble.

Any change from his normal behavior should be a warning sign. Is he dressing better these days? Forgetting things at the office? Going to the gym more often? Playing cards on Friday night? By keeping you occupied with the kids or feeling sorry that he's working so much, poor devil, he is hoping to deflect your suspicions regarding his paramour.

The most difficult men to catch in the act are the ones who travel for their work. Sorry, but every traveling sales rep we know to says that it's a piece of cake to find a woman in any town he needs to visit. Internet dating sites have opened up a wealth of opportunities for the man on the road. Candice says she doesn't know how a woman can marry a traveling man. She once dated a divorced man who traveled for a well-known company, inspecting their many stores around the country. He was honest with her when he finally decided to marry his hometown girlfriend (whom he also met on the internet), but he wanted to continue to see Candice whenever he came to her city after the wedding! Imagine being that wife, married to a man for less than a year, and he's *still* seeing his long-time hook-ups. Old habits die hard, or not at all, it seems.

Of course, you can always hire a private investigator to follow him if you can't or won't. They're expensive, but they can rather quickly provide indisputable evidence of an affair if that's what you need.

The folks at Advanced Surveillance Group have uncovered some interesting data about the cheating men they've tracked that might surprise you:

- Men are more likely to have affairs for the sexual experience alone, rather than for any emotional gratification.
- Men appear able to engage in infidelity without remorse and without feelings for their sexual partner-in-crime.

- Men crave feeling good, and will blame their wives for the lack of a "feel-good" vibe at home, giving themselves permission to seek it elsewhere.
- Our society seems to reward men who behave this way by linking power and money to men who are desired by women.
- Their ability to compartmentalize and cover their tracks leads men to be more successful at infidelity than women.
- Men are even *expected* to wander after being married for a number of years.

Is a private investigator really necessary? Not if you don't care what your man is doing. But if you have some suspicions, then, maybe yes, it could be necessary. Ministers, movie stars, and heads of governments (who have much more to lose if they're discovered) have cheated on their wives. Why would you think that your man wouldn't? If he can, he will. Opportunity or lack of it is the major variable.

Now, not all men are cheaters. And a PI can even clear your man if that's what the evidence shows. But you won't really know the truth about a guy unless you do your homework. Your man won't *tell you* he's being unfaithful unless he's ready to leave you for the other woman. And that is not the usual game plan most guys have in their heads. They typically just want to keep what they have at home and yet have something extra on the side. You're going to have to sniff around yourself. If you find out that, indeed, he always is where he says he is, you can relax a little. We say "a little" because, as you know, circumstances can change in the blink of an eye.

Further Reading

ASG: Advanced Surveillance Group, Inc.
http://www.cheatingspousepi.com/cheating_husband/

DeLorenzo, Anthony, and Dawn Ricci (2008). *Warning Signs: How to Know if Your Partner Is Cheating...and What to Do about It.* Guilford, CT:GPP Life.

"Love has been a battleground. They [men] *yearn* for warmth and kindness. In fact, the majority of divorced men who've hired me as their matchmaker tell me the *number one* thing they're looking for next tine around is **a nice person**."

~ Rachel Greenwald in *Have Him at Hello*

*"I saw her again last night,
And you know that I shouldn't
Just string her along; it's just not right.
If I couldn't I wouldn't,
But what can I do? I'm lonely too.
And it makes me feel so good to know
She'll never leave me. "*

> From "I Saw Her Again"
> by the Mamas and the Papas

11 • Does Anybody Ever Really Own Anybody?

The myth of the marital contract

"Your man." Can you ever really be sure that someone is "your man?"

Perhaps this is as good a time as any to broach a very delicate subject. As we all know, human ownership of another human being was abolished in 1863 by the Emancipation Proclamation. Therefore, any ideas you may have had concerning how you "own" this man whom you call your husband need to be discarded at once. Recent surveys even suggest that marriage itself is becoming less de rigueur as we move into the twenty-first century. And with more women willing to live with a man without benefit of marriage, men appear to be avoiding marriage more than ever, and successfully so. (George Clooney, are you reading this?)

For women who have married, a word of caution. With the divorce rate as high as it is, you need to consider your marriage contract a temporary business plan at best. One problem with marriage is that we like to think of it in terms of "forever." But all that does is delude us into believing we can stop working at it. We can't! We never can. We must treat every day like the first days of a new romance. Fan the flame, intensify the desire, provide the rewards that attracted our husbands into the marriage in the first place. If we are not doing that, then our husbands are going to get their intimacy needs met somewhere else by someone else. And the wife is always the last to know.

Put a little index card somewhere where you can read it every day: "NEVER STOP BEING THE DESIRABLE WOMAN HE MARRIED." Don't let him see it, but let it remind you that extreme and total vigilance is necessary every day. It's 9 pm. Do you really know where your husband is? Think about that the next time you have trouble reaching him on his cell.

Too much work just to keep your husband in your marital bed? Only you can answer that question. What we do know is that marriage counselors keep telling us how much effort a marriage requires. It should be apparent that they have been absolutely right.

Anne remembers a gift that her young salesman gave her: a lacy black teddy with red ribbons from Frederick's of Hollywood. He loves when she wears it for him. But she often wonders if he bought the same teddy for his girlfriend. Anne says that, in her experience, men tend to give the same gifts to their girlfriends that they give to their "other women" because they figure what works with one will work with the other. One thing is certain, once you find out that your man is cheating on you, you will see his gifts in a different light.

The young man Sylvia sees owns a home and several rental properties with his wife. No doubt the missus believes that all that joint property is a testament to the strength of their relationship. In fact, many women see the purchase of a home together as a sign that "this relationship is going to last."

Yet for other women, it takes a baby to seal the deal. Anne's young man had a baby boy with his ex-girlfriend, and he took his parental responsibilities very seriously. But his ex believed that she owned him because they had a child together. She would not tolerate his seeing other women. Even though they broke up a couple of years ago, she will still drive over to his house occasionally at 3:00 or 4:00 in the morning and create a noisy scene if she sees a strange car parked on his driveway. Alas, even a baby together does not confer ownership on one another. And drama won't do it either.

Sheila, who has a master's degree, has helped her young man write papers for his own MBA. She finds it peculiar that this very intelligent man has a wife who only finished high school, but there probably was great sexual chemistry present in the beginning which he assumed would continue forever, "till death do us part." Six years and two children later, the chemistry has changed. And his wife is not someone who is his intellectual equal. The relationship between a husband and wife is complicated and organic. It can morph dramatically over time, even though the parties involved do not will it to change. That is why men have occasionally been heard to remark, "I can't remember what I ever saw in her."

For some men, the disparity between whom they courted and who their wives turned out to be is a great disappointment. For others, over time, it is the wife who decides that her husband is no longer the man she thought she married. No one can control how another human being will change over time. Even though we may pledge our love forever, we can't be sure that we will be able to love one another unconditionally. As humans, we must constantly take and retake the temperature of our relationships. When we see that the fire is burning out, we must find ways to revive it, or accept the reality that the flame will be extinguished at some point.

Some writers have predicted the demise of the institution of marriage which they describe as an anachronism in this day and age. Certainly the failure of one out of every two marriages lends credibility to this prediction. Others, like Ashton Applewhite, fear that marriage itself can damage some people, particularly women. *In Cutting Loose: Why Women Who End Their Marriages Do So Well*, she writes, "Marriage reduces many women, who willingly, often unthinkingly, embrace a peculiarly circumscribed identity and set of priorities when they give up being single." No doubt the same could apply to some men.

Some of our cougars have expressed similar sentiments. One might suspect that the cougar is looking for a husband. But the cougars we spoke to cherish their freedom. All spoke disparagingly of their experiences within marriage.

Sylvia says marriage made her feel like a second-class citizen, a servant in her own house. Candice lived in fear that she would never measure up to what her husband expected a wife to be and do. Nina sensed that her husband was constantly comparing her to other women, and that she wasn't pretty enough, or smart enough, or artistic enough to compete with them. Sheila felt reduced to an administrative assistant in her own marriage. "He was the boss, made all the decisions. I was just there for clerical support." If marriage seemed like prison, or at least detention, for some, it's no wonder that many cougars aren't contemplating tying the knot again.

Young wives and girlfriends sometimes make the mistake of thinking that the ring they wear symbolizes their ownership of a man. If they convey that message to their husbands or boyfriends, they may only encourage the men to act out to prove them wrong. Neither men nor women "own" one another in marriage.

Anne says there is a fantasy of ownership that we carry in our minds, though. "I remember when I got divorced I felt bad because I thought I had owned my husband. We were married, so wasn't he mine? How dare someone take him from me! I think shattering that fantasy hurt more than losing my husband to another woman. I had nurtured the fantasy of having a man of my own since I was a girl. But now I know that no one owns anyone else."

The marriage ceremony gives couples an illusion of permanence. Previous generations of couples may have stayed together for religious or economic reasons, even when there was no love lost between spouses. But today's divorce rate shows that marriage ceremony is no guarantee of permanence in a relationship. Women can never assume that they own a man, no matter how long they've been together, how much property they jointly own, or how many kids they've got. Instead, they must keep finding ways to make their men *want to stay* in the relationship. If he'd rather be with you than anyone else, then you have a small measure of security. So figure out what your man wants, and be sure he gets it from you. Because that's about as close to ownership as anyone will get.

Further Reading

Applewhite, Ashton (1998). *Cutting Loose: Why Women Who End Their Marriages Do So Well.* NY:HarperCollins Publishers.

Greenwald, Rachel (2009). *Have Him at Hello.* NY:Three Rivers Press.

Statistics on Marriage from the US Census Bureau:

Americans Marrying Older, Living Alone More:
http://www.census.gov/newsroom/releases/archives/families_households/cb06-83.html (2006)

First Marriages That End in Divorce Average 8 yrs. in Length:
http://www.census.gov/newsroom/releases/archives/marital_status_living_arrangements/cb07-131.html (2007)

Increase in Cohabitation from 2009 to 2010:
http://www.census.gov/newsroom/releases/archives/families_households/2010-09_23_families_households.html

Men and Women Waiting Longer to Marry:
http://www.census.gov/newsroom/releases/archives/families_households/cb10-174.html (2010)

Straight from the Cougar's Mouth:

"Some women who have a good man don't treat him as well as they should. He should be Number One on their list, but he isn't. They won't get it till he's gone, and it'll be too late."

"The bottom line is that few people will avoid being personally touched by an affair. If not in your own relationship, you will almost certainly be affected through the experiences of a friend or family member. Since you are unlikely to avoid this issue, you are wise to be prepared in advance by having as much understanding as possible. It's very difficult to think clearly if you wait until you're in the midst of trying to deal with it."

~ Peggy Vaughan, *The Monogamy Myth: A Personal Handbook for Recovering from Affairs*

12 • Your Options Now That You Know

In his popular online relationship book for women, Catchhimandkeephim.com, Christian Carter teaches that there are six critical elements in a loving relationship with a man: attraction, commitment, sex, love, communication, and boundaries. We hear about the first five quite often, but it's that sixth one – boundaries – that can cause a great deal of trouble between partners.

Candice relates how her husband seemed to have trouble with boundaries from the beginning of their relationship:

Sometimes he would tell me about conversations he'd had at work with some of the women in his department. They became quite graphic and seemed to me to cross the line between friendly and downright intimate. I asked him why he would participate in such conversations which to me seemed totally inappropriate. He laughed and said, "Not at all. We're just kidding around."

Besides placing himself in a dangerous position (someone could accuse him of sexual harassment), my husband was violating a bond I thought we had with one another: a bond that makes our intimate talk and activities private, something we share only with each other. And I was shocked to find that he was talking to a woman in his department about extremely intimate sexual things. It was at that point that I realized he had very poorly defined boundaries, if he had any boundaries at all. And they didn't end with conversations. They extended into actions. I suddenly realized that he had no understanding of boundaries at all.

Candice discovered how important it is to really know one's partner before making an important commitment like marriage. That is why in earlier times, and even today in some cultures, a courtship period has a required lengthy time span. This gives the couple and their families time to get to know one another really well before tying the knot.

In our society, with the postponement of marriage becoming more and more common, women often find themselves near the end of their reproductive years and panicking that they may not marry in time to have a family. In their panic, many marry men they do not know very well.

Just as Candice would have benefited from having more awareness of her boyfriend's problem with boundaries, so do many women rush into marriage without knowing what they're getting into. Once the boundaries have been crossed, the problem becomes what to do about it.

There really are only three options. You can divorce (or leave one another if you're not married) if the transgression is just too painful or intolerable for you to bear. You can enlist the aid of a trusted third party and begin counseling to see if the rift can be repaired. Or you can accept one another's differences and decide to live with them. Some people call this an open marriage, although it rarely is as open for both partners as it is for one. No one can tell you what is right for you. You both must reach a decision.

Candice discovered her husband was cheating with his colleague at work. He claimed it was a natural extension of their work friendship and the feelings they had developed for each other. He saw no reason to terminate the marriage, but he also saw no reason to terminate the affair. He would have liked for both to go on. Candice could not accept the continuation of the affair and filed for divorce.

Once she was free, Candice realized that there were many men like David who couldn't see where the marriage ended and where the affair began. Everything was working for *them*, so what was all the fuss about? These men tried to keep their affairs separate from their home lives, except where financial decisions sometimes impacted their family's lifestyle. (Candice's husband paid for the painting and decorating of his girlfriend's apartment with family money.)

Some men are so accustomed to having women do things for them (thank you, Mrs. Mother-in-law!) that when women outside their primary relationship offer to do things for them (teach them Spanish, introduce them to tennis, cook them their favorite paella), they don't realize that they are crossing boundaries that shouldn't be crossed. The old teachings of the Catholic

Church termed this "putting oneself in the occasion of sin." In other words, asking for trouble.

Candice has a friend, Rose, whose husband didn't even try to separate his affair from his family life. He actually asked Rose if she would teach his girlfriend how to cook the fabulous dishes Rose prepared at home! In Rose's and Candice's cases, these men were oblivious to the blurring of sensitive boundaries. Even counseling wasn't able to make them realize how hurtful and damaging their behaviors were.

Rose divorced and eventually remarried, happily, but Candice went on to become a cougar herself. How could she? She explains:

I dated plenty after my divorce, and I found so many men with excuses for their bad behavior that I finally began to believe that all the good ones really were already taken and not even on the market. Making the best of a not-so-good situation, I decided to just get what I needed and hope that someday a Mr. Wonderful would land in my lap. It hasn't happened yet, but in the meantime I have had a pretty fair sex life, have the freedom to come and go as I please, and I'm flattered that men still find me attractive. I wish my marriage had worked out, but I knew what I could and couldn't tolerate, and so I did what I had to do. I still hope to find a good guy before I die. But I have to admit, I'm not very trusting any more.

This, then, is the problem that you face if your husband is seeing another woman. Do you divorce? Do you turn a blind eye? Do you get counseling? What if there are children? Does that change your decision? The answer depends as much on who you are as a person as on who your husband is.

For some men, a little more excitement in their lives is all they need to stay put. Often husbands did not realize how much having a child would change their lives, and now that they know, they are disillusioned. Children have a tendency to turn a home into a child-centered environment. A wife who can help put that excitement back into the marriage stands a very good chance of keeping her husband from looking elsewhere for his satisfaction. Excitement can mean whatever your husband wants it to mean, so you need to get his definition. Is it skydiving? Motocross racing? Sex in new and unusual places? His definition may be different from yours, so it's best to define terms at the outset, before making any changes. You want him to look forward to coming home to you.

Once you know his terms, you can try to be that exciting partner he wants. A word of caution, though: things don't always work out as planned. Jeri Ryan, the actress, decided that her husband's fascination with visiting sex clubs in various cities around the world and performing sexual acts in front of others was a dealbreaker.

(There may of course have been other issues as well that were sealed by the court.) She divorced him, and the resulting negative publicity cost Jack Ryan a Senate seat and his political career. Their son will one day learn the facts behind his parents' divorce. Their story ends with a messy finale to what looked, in the beginning, like a fairy tale romance between two of the planet's beautiful people.

Nena and George O'Neill, in their famous book on *Open Marriage* (1972), wrote: "We are not recommending outside sex, but we are not saying it should be avoided either. The choice is entirely up to you." Although they seemed to be promoting extramarital affairs, the O'Neills later insisted that they felt fidelity was just as valid a choice. What you do in the face of infidelity will be a very personal decision that only you can make.

Anne remembers meeting an older couple (in their 60s) at a BDSM club she attended a few times with her younger man. The husband and wife had both been married before, but they found in each other the same definitions of excitement that they had failed to find in their previous partners. Anne would advise wives and girlfriends to feel out their partner's kinkiest sex fantasies, because those are the ones that will ultimately cause problems ahead if there are going to be any problems. Just as a woman needs to know if her fiance drinks to excess, and a man needs to know if his intended is addicted to painkillers, both parties should be aware of one another's most deep-seated sexual preferences as well.

Famous people and just plain nobodies, male and female, from every walk of life, have made the choice to take lovers outside of their marriages, so we know the desire to be unfaithful can be very strong. But some couples are able to tolerate a certain amount of infidelity in their partners. If you are one of those couples, then other people's choices shouldn't deter you. Most couples, however, probably have more difficulty surviving infidelity.

On the other hand, as Dan Savage writes, if your non-open marriage is already headed for divorce, an open marriage might save it. The worst that could happen is you'd eventually get a divorce, which you were preparing to do anyway.

Every choice we make, as partners, though, must be weighed carefully. We must be sure we are being honest with ourselves and each other, and that we are both on the same page with our choices. What is the right decision for one couple may not be right for another. Only the couple themselves can make that call, but they will benefit from the guidance and clarification offered by a couples therapist or a marriage counselor.

Further Reading

Nena and George O'Neill (1973). *Open Marriage: A New Lifestyle for Couples*. London: Peter Owen.

Savage Love, advice column by Dan Savage:
www.thestranger.com/**savage**

Vaughan, Peggy (2003). *The Monogamy Myth: A Personal Handbook for Recovering from Affairs (Third Edition)*. NY:Newmarket Press.

Ask Yourself:

- Do I ever leave him alone for long periods of time, like when I take my mother shopping?
- Does he seem to have reasons to leave the house in the evening (Home Depot, the bank, etc.) while I'm occupied with something else?
- Do I sometimes nag him so much that he has actually left the house to get away from me?

Straight from the Cougar's Mouth:

"You know what will drive him fastest into the arms of another woman? Drama. Men hate drama."

"Unfortunately, men change the most after a relationship ends – or after a career failure. And few men – or women, for that matter – can change personality patterns that are fundamental to them."

~ Warren Farrell, *Why Men Are the Way They Are*

13 • Ten Talks You Must Have with Your Man (or Your Next Man)

(Preferably *before* you move in, marry, or have a baby.)

Most human couplings occur on the basis of very superficial compatibilities. They like the same movies and music, they're both from Boston, they were both raised Jewish. But the real problems in marriage usually arise from some very deeply held beliefs about how couples should behave toward one another and toward others. Sure, it's great when both love Mexican food and skiing in Colorado, but that will never hold together a couple who have very serious relationship problems.

Unfortunately, the talks recommended in this chapter almost never occur in the haze of romantic love. One of you will need to clear your head and, yes, say, "We have to talk." Of course, you *can* talk over Mexican food, if that helps. And the talks should *not* take place all in an afternoon. These are conversations meant to reveal your true selves to one another. They aren't meant to be a "grilling" or interrogation. So try and space them out over several weeks or months of dating.

1. What's your definition of **monogamy** and **faithfulness**? Is there any kind of relationship that your partner might have with another person that you're not crazy about? Emotional closeness? Same sex activity friendships? Strangers online? How much time do each of you expect to spend away from each other with certain friends? One boys' night out per week? How about three? Do you want to be monogamous/faithful? Why or why not? How would that work? What would be the rules? What if the rules were broken? What if either one of you changes your mind about being monogamous/faithful? Do you then come clean and make an

announcement? What will you do if your relationship stops being satisfying to either one of you?
2. What would be a **deal-breaker** for each of you in your relationship? In other words, what would make you say "This is over"? Alcoholism? Weight gain? Loss of interest in sex? Obsession with work or pastime? Think hard. Be thorough. Would a divorce or break-up inevitably follow? Or counseling?
3. How do you feel about **marriage**? Do you want to be married? Why or why not? Does marriage signify exclusivity? What sort of definition do you have in your head? What do you think about extra-marital affairs in marriage? How about one-night stands? When would they be justified? Would living together satisfy you as much as being married? Why or why not?
4. What about **prostitution**, or sex-for-money? Have you ever paid for sex? If so, would you do it again? Under what circumstances? Does visiting a prostitute constitute infidelity? Or is it acceptable because there's no emotional involvement? Do you expect to visit prostitutes in the future? Under what circumstances?
5. How do **children** fit into your life? Do you want to have children? Why or why not? If yes, how many? How do you feel

about adoption? Blended families? Can you accept living with/caring for your partner's children from another relationship? How about shared custody visitations? What kinds of child-care arrangements do you foresee? What child-related problems are you most fearful of? Which relationship do you think will be number one in your life? The parent-child relationship or the partner-partner relationship?

6. If marriage and/or children are not in your future, what do you see as the **benefits** resulting from your being a couple? What do you hope to get from this relationship? Friendship? Companionship? Regular sex and intimacy? Shared financial and household responsibilities? A better quality of life? What if those benefits cease to exist for you? What happens then?

7. How does **sex** fit into your life? How much/how often do you need it? What kinds of sex do you desire (be specific)? Are you bi-curious? Have you ever had a homosexual relationship? What is the kinkiest thing you want to do? Would you consider sex clubs, or partner swapping, or "the lifestyle"? What fetishes do you indulge in or would like to indulge in? Do you enjoy certain sex practices that you think might be an issue for your partner?

What are they? Where do you draw the line in sex practices? What will you do if you start to disagree on these issues?

8. How do you feel about **control**? Are males and females equal? Do you respect members of the opposite sex? Do you think men and women are different (besides in the obvious ways)? If so, how? Do men and women want the same things out of life? Do you both want the same things out of life? Are men or women better suited to certain kinds of responsibilities than others? Be specific. In what way would control enter into your relationship? Should one person in a relationship (say, the man) always have the final word on a question or decision? Would either of you ever control certain decision-making arenas or perhaps control the other's freedom to behave in certain ways? Finances? Child-rearing? Where to live? How? What kinds of division of labor and division of authority could you both tolerate? What could not be tolerated? Should a man ever have the right to strike a woman? When? Should a woman ever have the right to strike a man? When?

9. How do you feel about **lying**? Do you sometimes lie to get your own way, or to cover your tracks, or to avoid consequences, or to manipulate people? Does

everybody lie? How would you feel if your partner lied to you for any of these reasons? What would be the consequences of lying to each other? Under what circumstances do you feel it is all right to lie? Do either of you have a history of lying in the past? Under what circumstances did that occur?
10. What about **religion**? Do you believe in a god or supreme being of some sort? How do you describe or define that god? What if your partner has very different beliefs from yours? Are you members of the same or different religious denominations? Can you see maintaining your religious affiliations throughout your relationship? Or will one partner need to "convert" to the other's religion? If there are children, how will they be reared regarding religion? In-laws? Do you anticipate friction from in-laws regarding your religious views? How will that be handled? Do you believe that certain rules for human behavior came from a higher power? Or do we humans decide the rules?

These questions only just begin to scratch the surface of what you two should be discussing. You should know about one another's backgrounds, your families' histories, medical conditions and predispositions, any criminal or legal problems that either of you has experienced, and as much sexual history as you can reasonably discuss. Each partner has a right to know who he/she is marrying, since beyond being a romantic relationship, this is also a legal partnership. You wouldn't want to invest in a business with someone you barely knew, right? So why marry a virtual stranger?

Further Reading

Farrell, Warren (1986). *Why Men Are the Way They Are.* NY: Berkley Books.

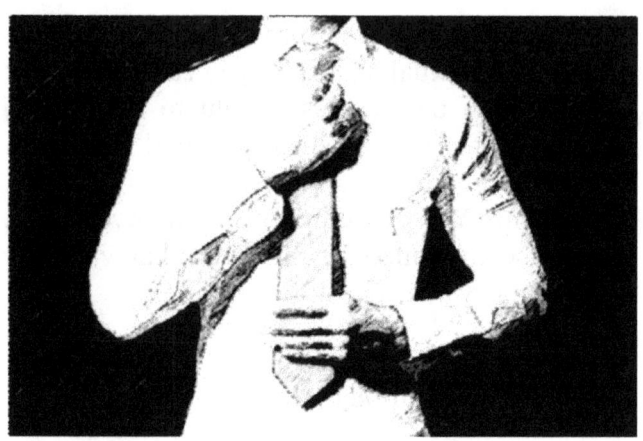

Nine Things You Need to Know about Your Guy:

1

He wishes you'd initiate sex more often than just on his birthday. A lot more often.

2

He needs his ego stroked a lot more than you think. His confidence is shaky.

3

He'd love to have sex with other women but he doesn't want to hurt you.

4

Sex is his solution for many problems: worry, anxiety, stress. And also his reward for his successes.

5

His job is a huge part of his identity. Be careful how you talk about his job. You're talking about him.

6

Relationships are difficult for him. He's not always sure what to say to your mother or your girlfriends. Or you.

7

He's torn between treating you as an equal and controlling you. Sometimes he doesn't know which feels right to him.

8

He loves to see you all dressed up, feminine. It doesn't happen nearly often enough for him.

9

He really craves more excitement in his life. The adrenaline gives him a rush he can't get any other way. So he rides a motorcycle and likes to take chances.

Straight from the Cougar's Mouth:

"I don't think he'll ever stop cheating on his wife. He's had so many women in his past that for him variety has become a way of life. I think he probably ruined himself for monogamy a long time ago."

"Simply said, your husband needs sex – and he needs you to love it too."

~ Dr. Kevin Leman,
7 Things He'll Never Tell You

14 • What's in It for the Cougar?

By now, you're probably wondering what the cougar gets out of all this. After all, she says she's not interested in marrying your guy, so what's the point?

One thing all the cougars I spoke to agreed upon: They all loved sex, and they liked being with the men they saw. The men, of course, are getting something from the relationship as well, or they would not be hanging around for long. Sex is probably tops on the list. The young man/older woman pairing is definitely a kind of symbiotic relationship, with each party bringing something of value to the table.

There are several points worth mentioning here. Although different women find different reasons for seeing younger men, there are a few reasons that come up again and again in conversations with older women. Here are the most often-mentioned justifications from cougars themselves.

Hot sex with a younger man. Pretty obvious, huh? But many older women did not experiment much back when they were younger, and so they have only the foggy memories of their once-young husbands to reminisce over. Sex with your guy gives the cougar another body to fantasize about when she's alone. Many cougars regret that they were "good girls" when younger themselves and therefore do not have a lot of memories of hot, young partners. The time spent now with younger men fills those gaps nicely. And the newly-made memories are much fresher and easier to access, too. You may not think your man is hot or sexy, but the older woman does.

As time ages us, women are expected to maintain their youthful faces and figures as much as possible. But men are forgiven many of their overindulgences, and they don't rush off to the cosmetic surgeon to correct perceived flaws. Consequently, the cougar may find that men her own age are not as attractive to her as your man is. They've let themselves go. An affair with a younger man is a means for her to recapture the thrill of sex with a hot body.

Sheila has a goal: She wants to fuck fifty different men before she dies. She's up to forty-three right now, so she's getting close. And she wants the men to be men she really desires. No more pity sex. She believes that when women are freed from the bonds of an exclusive relationship like marriage, their desires become more congruent with men's desires. But their pool of available partners shrinks as they grow older.

Regular sex, without resorting to one-night stands. Some cougars have decided that regular sex is something they want in their lives, and finding the right available man is often difficult when their age-mates all seem to be married or attached. Regular sex has health benefits as well as psychological benefits. The older woman who has made the decision to keep her sex life alive may have few other options than to sleep with younger men. Of course, the dynamics work in her favor: most younger men complain they aren't getting enough sex, so finding a woman who wants it appeals to them as well.

When Anne was young, she made a conscious decision to try to get married by twenty-five and have her children by thirty-five. She was able to make that happen, but then she divorced at 45. Her penchant for planning, or time-lining, her life didn't go away after her divorce. She made a conscious decision to continue having sex. She wanted to experience things she hadn't experienced in her marriage, and she also wanted to keep her sex drive alive and well in case she did find a man she'd want to be with for the long haul. Again, Anne has been able to make that happen.

Candice also wants to feed her sex drive, but mainly for the health benefits that she feels she derives from regular sex. Although she's not a big contributor to causes, Candice "services" one police officer at least once a week. "I don't think our men who put their lives on the line for us day after day should have to wonder where their next piece of ass is coming from," she says. "I can't take care of the whole police force, but I do my small part." She claims she would do the same for a firefighter or an Afghan vet.

Validation that she is still desirable. As the cougar ages, doubts enter her mind (as they may enter all women's minds) concerning her sexual desirability. The older woman is as vulnerable as any woman to the pressures of the media and its demand for youth and beauty. By pairing with a younger man, she dispels, at least in part, some of those doubts.

Most men will not continue to have unsatisfactory sex, time and time again. Although the old adage, "Bad sex is better than no sex at all," may be true, the average man is likely to seek out better sex if he can get it. The cougar reasons that if a man continues to see her, she must still be desirable and still able to provide a satisfying sexual experience. This kind of validation is important to someone who sees her youth and beauty diminishing over time. Nina says, "I know if he comes back again and again, I still have some appeal in the sexual marketplace."

Opportunity to continue thinking young. Lest you think his body is all she craves, you should know that his mind is also of great interest to the cougar. If the older woman doesn't have younger men (and women) to communicate with, she runs the risk of settling into "old thinking," missing out on the new perspectives of events and life itself. Younger generations think differently about many issues, and keeping in touch with your younger man helps the cougar keep fresh ideas and insights in mind. This not only keeps her feeling younger, but it may offer advantages in her work and other areas of her life.

Call it the Dracula Syndrome, but young blood and new ideas are vital to an active life. The older woman keeps up-to-date on technology, music, movies, and books by sharing ideas with your guy. It's a give-and-take, in which her perspectives are valued just as much as his.

Novel venues and experiences. You may think your life is routine, maybe even boring, but the older woman sees adventure and newness in the activities your man engages in. She is thrilled to be able to share them, even occasionally, as they open doors that she might not otherwise enter.

Anne visited a nudist resort in Florida with her young man and learned about several different lifestyles that were popular with people they met there. Sylvia became actively involved in a theater group after observing a few acting classes with her partner. Other cougars have taken up new hobbies or even new careers based on experiences they first shared with younger men. They might never have been exposed to those opportunities had they not been involved with those men.

Older women are sometimes asked to accompany men on business trips or holidays when wives or girlfriends cannot attend. These opportunities for travel – with a partner – are almost always enjoyable.

Personal care and fitness take on renewed importance. Because the older woman feels (rightly or wrongly) that her body is being compared to those of younger women, being involved with a younger man keeps her more conscious of her appearance.

One woman, 63 years old as this goes to press, visits the gym five days a week and keeps her weight to a trim 125 lbs. – the same weight she was when she was first married. She has her hair done professionally and gets manicures and pedicures regularly. She attributes this diligence to the fact that her partners are all twenty to thirty years younger than she is! Needless to say, she doesn't have trouble attracting men her own age, either, since she looks very good compared to other women of sixty-three.

Many women forget what visual creatures men really are. As they become involved in marriage and family matters, women often neglect the very visual components that attracted their men to them. The cougar keeps up her appearance, and it pays dividends in her sex life and her career as well.

Sheila, who works in a busy law firm, has seen many of her female colleagues go from slender, cute and vivacious to chubby, bossy and crabby as they marry, settle down, and have babies. She knows their husbands have noticed it too. As unfair as it may seem, women are *always* competing with other women, even long after they have that ring on their finger.

Too often, women see marriage as the end-game, the point at which they have won the competition and no longer need to worry about their man. They think he is theirs. But with the divorce rate at 50%, it doesn't take a genius to understand that men keep looking. Even marriage doesn't prevent them from checking out "what's out there," as they like to say. And if they see something "out there" that attracts them, they will go for it.

The opportunity exists to benefit from hindsight. Although she can't go back and do-over a part of her past life, being with your man is a form of life therapy for the older woman. She can see, in your mistakes, her own mistakes of the past and in a sense relive some of those times and make different choices this time around. She also is able to synthesize knowledge from her past with her present in an effort to understand men in general. Needless to say, they're a puzzle to many women.

Sylvia says that being with a younger man reminds her of her own marriage, and how confused she was sometimes about her husband's wants and desires. She now has an opportunity to test out alternative behaviors and feels she has a better understanding of men in general. She can't go back and have a marriage do-over. That's impossible. But she can use her newfound wisdom with her younger partner.

How do cougars select their partners? Candice reminds us that it is the men who make the first move – they make the selection. But out of all the men who make advances, whom do the cougars decide to see?

Here again, each woman is different. Sheila says she always goes for the handsomest hunk. She never attracted handsome guys in her own youth, so now she has the opportunity to see what that's like. And she does like it.

Candice looks for good sex. If a young man is not adventurous, or is only looking out for his own satisfaction at the expense of hers, he will become history in short order. She admits she is attracted to "bad boys," but will not make the initial overture. She wants him to seduce her, to be sure that he is attracted to her, first, before she plunges ahead into a relationship with him. "If you make the first move," Candice says, "you may end up with a one-night stand. Practically no man will turn you down, of course, but it has to be his idea if it's going to last a while. That's why I always let them make the first move."

Nina likes a man who has time for dinner and conversation. She knows that most attached men do not want to be seen in public with their other woman out of fear of discovery. But if a man orders dinner delivered and remembers to bring some wine, the "date" feeling is present and that satisfies her. Add a little intellectual stimulation, and Nina is happy.

Anne has stricter rules for herself these days. No married men with small children (they can't keep to a schedule), no men seeing multiple women (admittedly hard to know), and no one under thirty (too immature). Her limits have been determined over the past ten years with many younger men, and, for her at least, these limitations provide the best experience.

Sylvia enjoys going out, so she prefers a young man who is not attached. But she has found ways to go out with her attached men, too. She can pretend to be a client, or they can meet at places he and his friends and significant other do not frequent. Sylvia knows that the relationship must be on the down-low, and that's the way she plays it.

All is not rosy for cougars, however. Every one interviewed for this book has suffered some cognitive dissonance as a result of her experiences. These women obviously like men. They want to keep men in their lives, in their beds. But they also have learned that being with a man usually means leaving oneself open to betrayal, no matter how hard the woman in the relationship may try to be all things to her man. Cougars believe that there are some faithful husbands in the world, but they never meet them! The men they meet do not view sex or commitment – perhaps not even *honesty* -- the same way their women do. That creates a problem for the cougars too.

If men keep secrets from their wives, they will keep secrets from the cougar as well.

If they lie to their girlfriends, they will lie to the cougar as well.

If they cheat on their significant others, they will cheat on the cougar as well. Maybe with another cougar!

Some men are simply not cut out for a committed relationship, because of their own selfishness or through habits they've developed over their lives.

The main difference between the wife and the cougar is that the cougar knows what she's involved in and has made the choice herself. Most wives and girlfriends don't have any idea what their men are up to.

Occasionally, the cougar's emotions get out of hand too. Try as she might to keep emotions out of the picture, sometimes an older woman will begin to fall for her younger man, even though a serious relationship would be most unlikely to develop. Sylvia shared her strategy for dealing with that kind of situation:

"I tell myself that what he's doing would be hurtful if his wife or girlfriend knew. I tell myself that he would do the same thing to me, if we were in a committed relationship, that he's doing to her. I would not be able to change his stripes any more than his wife or girlfriend can. His desire for infinite variety would always win.

"A long time ago, a friend of mine had a small monkey as a pet. While she loved this little monkey, she complained endlessly about all the mischief he got into, the things he broke around the house, the times when he refused to cooperate with her for no apparent reason at all. Just plain orneriness. Even keeping him in his cage (a very large one, for those who may be wondering) when he was being particularly obnoxious didn't help, because he would resort to making so much noise that the neighbors would complain. One of our mutual friends finally said, 'But Carmen, he's a *monkey*. What did you expect? That he'd behave like some choirboy?' And my friend answered, sadly, 'I guess I thought that if he lived with me, and I fed him and treated him well, he would be glad to behave by my rules. But it sure didn't turn out that way.'

"Needless to say, as much as she loved him, my friend Carmen eventually had to give the monkey away to an animal refuge, because she just couldn't live with what, for him, was normal behavior."

Although men and women do belong to the same species, there are enough differences between them in brain behavior, socialization, and societal roles that we might as well come from different species. To paraphrase Sylvia's friend, "But he's a *man*. What did you expect?" We women have to learn how to look for behavior that we know may be happening behind our backs. Why? Because they *are* men. And if our searches turn up nothing, then we should cherish them all the more.

So is there something about these cougars' men that their wives or girlfriends failed to see? Some warning sign that this could happen?

Sheila says no. In fact, almost every man that she and the other cougars have had relationships with are exactly the kind of man that they would have wanted their daughters to meet: good looking, successful in their chosen careers, and, on the surface, at least, very kind and considerate. Yet, each one is betraying the one person who should mean the most to him: his significant other. How can we explain that?

Some writers with a biological or anthropological bent like to explain men's resistance to monogamy as a part of his genetic inheritance, a propensity to spread his seed among many females to insure that the species survives. But why then turn his attention to an older woman who is no longer in her childbearing years? That makes no sense.

It's clearly not about procreation, or survival of the species in the case of the older woman. Men's needs can be as varied as women's, but men simply don't look at sex the same way women do. Certainly there are some women who cheat on their husbands or simply can't say no to an attractive man. But this book is about a cultural phenomenon known as the cougar, and to understand why she even exists requires that we understand the motivations of men who seek her out.

Americans, as a cultural group, fail to recognize how important sex is to men. Wives in our culture are not prepped for marriage by their mothers in the same way that women in other cultures may be. We are very vanilla, very naïve, in our thinking. If men in Arabian countries are brought up with images of sheiks and harems, if men from Latin cultures like to view themselves as Don Juans, if African tribal leaders always have the privilege of deflowering young women within their tribes, and if Europeans have always routinely kept mistresses on the side, how can we deny that sex is supremely important to men? We may as well be ostriches, burying our heads in the sand. The truth is all around us: Men are extremely sexual beings. Almost every man, if pressed, will admit that he doesn't get enough sex. Or enough of the kind of sex he craves.

Playgirl magazine has never been as successful as *Playboy* or other men's glossy magazines. Women may attend a male strip show once or twice in their lives, but that usually satisfies their curiosity for all time. And who would even know where to look for a heterosexual male prostitute? (American gigolo, where are you now?) Sex as a drive is far more alive and well among men than among women. But therein lies the rub: if a man and woman are to spend a lifetime together, they must work on making sure that neither partner's needs go unmet.

Of course, there is no guarantee that being super-sexual yourself will hold your man. Many famous female sex-objects throughout history had their problems with men as well. Even Pamela Anderson and Halle Berry can't seem to hold onto a man for long. Perhaps that has more to do with other traits than their sexual appetites. And the men involved may have issues that make them unsuitable for long-term partners. But to make the most of your admittedly nothing-like-Hollywood relationship, you *must* consider your man's sexual satisfaction. Not to do so would be tantamount to asking for trouble.

See the next chapter for ideas that come straight from men.

Further Reading

Kerner, Ian (2006). *He Comes Next.* NY:William Morrow.

Kerner, Ian (2010). *She Comes First.* NY:Harper Paperbacks.

Zilbergeld, Bernie (1999). *The New Male Sexuality.* NY:Bantam Books.

"If they were sure that their wives or girlfriends would never uncover their infidelities, many men would have sex with other women. That's the ugly truth.

~ Gerstman, Pizzo, and Seldes,
What Men Want

15 • The Sex Your Man Wants

If you suspect your guy is seeing a cougar, then something must be missing from your relationship which she is able to provide. It is probably a certain type of sex, or a specific sex act, or simple variety, although other factors (which have been mentioned in previous chapters) may also be motivating him to stray.

Our cougars have identified some sexual practices that they have provided which seem to be in demand among the younger men they see. You may not want to contemplate all of them, but you may wish to begin to incorporate some of them (gradually, not all at once), at least the ones that your man appears to crave most. Doing so may require a change in your own thinking about sex, but change is probably necessary if you are to bring him back to you exclusively.

Other factors, such as your personality, the qualities of your home, your intellectual compatibility, common life goals, etc., should also be considered, as any of these factors may also be the stimulus that sends your man into the arms of an older woman.

Frequency of sex. You've read it before, over and over, that compromise is necessary. If he wants it twelve times a week and you're satisfied with three, then you two should reach a suitable compromise. This advice is patently wrong! If your man wants it twelve times a week, he will GET it twelve times a week, one way or another. YOU must be the one providing those sexual encounters, or it will be someone else. Seems unfair? Maybe it is. But it is a fact. If you cannot see your way to twelve times a week, then perhaps he is not the man for you. Or you are not the woman for him. Better decide how badly you want to keep him.

It's been said before, but it warrants repeating here: Sex, for men, is an inelastic demand. As a general rule, they want more of it than women do, and they want more variety as well. Unless a man is choosing a woman because she is wealthy, or because she can advance his career, he is choosing her largely because she provides the kind of sexual experiences he craves – *craves* – on a regular basis.

In their now classic book, *What Men Want*, Gerstman, Pizzo and Seldes advise, "Every man has a favorite position. And it is important to a man that his partner is pleased and pleases him in this favored position. For him, that spells compatibility." For some men, that may mean anal sex with the woman on all fours and the man thrusting behind her. Other men may favor the position known as "sixty-nine." For still others, the woman must be roped and tied like a rodeo calf and fucked in that helpless state. Make no mistake about it. Once you find out what your man's favorite position is, it will be on the menu all the time. Without it, your man cannot be totally satisfied.

Dom or sub? Is he the dominant partner, or are you? How does he prefer it? If, like some men, your guy wants you to dominate him in the bedroom, at least some of the time, then you must learn how to function as a capable dominatrix. If, on the other hand, your man expects you to be submissive, at least once in a while, then you need to learn to be a suitable sex slave. As distasteful as this may sound to you at first, this kind of accommodation is exactly what demonstrates to your man that you love and appreciate him. In a healthy relationship, you should be able to ask for your needs to be met as well, without embarrassment or awkwardness. Fortunately, living in the times we do, there are plenty of books and DVDs available to help you in your quest for knowledge. You can and should take advantage of these resources to strengthen your bond with one another. With a little diligence on your part, Amazon.com can save your relationship!

Some dom/sub relationships require specific equipment, such as whips or riding crops, hoods, handcuffs or other sexual paraphernalia. It is imperative that you learn to use – and enjoy – these accoutrements of sex with your man if this is his cup of tea. With the many internet sites today catering to multiple sexual lifestyles, it will not be difficult for him to find someone who will fulfill his needs if you won't.

Even some sex advice columnists like Dan Savage will suggest that you allow your significant other to visit a dominatrix (or find a submissive, if that is his preference), but few couples can withstand the involvement of a third party, particularly when that party is of interest to only one of the partners. Better that *you* learn the role that fulfills your guy's needs. You may even find that you enjoy it. Our advice: Do everything you can to LEARN to enjoy it.

Threesomes and Foursomes. Some men, especially those who have already pushed the envelope to its seeming limits, will have developed a taste for more people in the room than just two. These days, men and women can join sex clubs or other specialty clubs (spanking, BDSM, swapping, etc.) which supply the kinds of experiences they seek. Your guy may want you to participate with him.

One would hope that he makes these predilections known to you before you exchange wedding bands, but if not, you would be wise to go with him to see if these clubs are something you can learn to enjoy with him. Many men are drawn to these sorts of clubs, where sexual acts are performed in front of others. (Some men like to be watched.) The clubs usually don't allow single men (known as "rogue males") because they tend to be aggressive and unpredictable. But they welcome single women, often admitting them for only a nominal fee. The sex club is usually a safe environment for trying something new, like adding a new partner, and many of the members are regulars who can show you the ropes.

If your husband or boyfriend wants to add a new "member" to your party of two, it will likely be another woman (although not necessarily, as we shall see shortly). You will need to be comfortable watching him having sex with this woman, and you may be required to have girl-on-girl sex with her as well for his enjoyment.

Some men like to add another man to the mix. They get aroused and often can cum watching their wife or girlfriend being fucked by another man. If your man also has some bisexual interest, he may want to penetrate (or be penetrated by) the other man. Some men just like to have their wives watch while they give or receive oral sex with a male partner.

Asian countries, Japan and Thailand in particular, are well known for providing outlets for the many varieties of sexual desires that men have. These may not be legal outlets, but they are readily available to men with the money to pay for them. Image rooms, for example, can simulate a crowded subway train, where men may stand among lovely young women and grope them. Almost any fantasy imaginable can be reproduced here. No doubt your man has read about them if he hasn't actually visited the Far East.

The kinds of sex your partner desires can only be discovered through open and honest communication with one another. Perhaps you have a sexual preference that you haven't mentioned to him? This would be an ideal conversation in which to bring it up.

BDSM. Bondage, discipline, domination, submission, sadism and masochism are acquired tastes. If your man is seriously into one of these lifestyles, he should have told you long before you became exclusive. If this is a late development in his life, you may want to try a few meetings at a BDSM club to see where, if at all, your interests lie. Because BDSM is not mainstream, this may be a stumbling block for the two of you. Try to determine how crucial this factor is to your guy's satisfaction. If he requires a partner who shares his preferences in this arena, you will need to explore what you find appealing. (It's not enough to simply *tolerate* a BDSM activity. You must really enjoy it for your partner to be satisfied.)

Should You Do Everything He Wants? Not all sexual practices are good for the marriage bond, particularly those which introduce additional people. There is always the possibility that you or your partner will become strongly attracted to one of those additional people, to the detriment of your own bond. However, men's sexual appetites being what they are, it is probably better for a wife or girlfriend to at least experiment to see what she can accept. If she doesn't accompany him, she will know that he is satisfying those desires without her, sometime, somewhere. You can take that to the bank.

Some men are thrill-seekers when it comes to motorcycles or single-engine planes. Others gamble the family farm on financial investments that are less than sound. If your man likes to push the envelope sexually, wanting to try activities that you seriously feel will hurt your bond with him, you have the right to refuse. Just realize that this type of man *will get what he wants* in the end, with or without you.

Other special requests that cougars have indulged which make their men come back for more:

- High heels, sheer or fishnet hose, lingerie and other sexy accessories;
- Ejaculation on a woman's face, breasts, or ass; ejaculate from masturbation, saved in a cup all day, which the woman will drink, enthusiastically, to show her appreciation;
- Body-scratching, head to toe or just on selected body parts, such as the back, head, or ass; rimming and ass-licking, sometimes to orgasm;
- Infantilization, in which the man may wear a diaper and suckle at the woman's breast; diaper-changing is also sometimes requested;

- Getting high together, on marijuana, alcohol, poppers or other substances; having specific kinds of sex while under the influence of these substances;
- Specific scenarios, such as rape, bondage, or prostitute sex; sex with a woman who dresses and pretends to be a child; sex with a woman in a specific uniform;
- Urination, man-on-woman and woman-on-man; drinking one another's urine;
- Sex in semi-public places, such as the office, a restaurant bathroom, the car or limousine;
- Talking dirty, using extremely graphic language in bed.

Gerstman, Pizzo and Seldes emphasize that when it comes to sex, a man is not able to make adjustments to his needs, like a woman might. For men, sex the way they like it *is* the bottom line.

One more note: A friend of ours was married to a man who "came out of the closet" while married. She tried valiantly to accept the changes in his behavior until the rejection and isolation she felt threatened her own well-being. Other women we know could not tolerate certain BDSM activities their husbands required. Should anything like this occur in your committed relationship, you will need a competent therapist to help you through what can be a traumatic and life-altering breakup experience. A good therapist is worth whatever the cost.

When a partner's behaviors (sexual or otherwise) become something you cannot comfortably live with, then your relationship should not continue. It is vitally important that a woman not lose herself in the effort to keep her man. The same advice would hold for a man desperately trying to keep a woman in his life.

Further Reading

Gerstman, Bradley, Christopher Pizzo, and Rich Seldes (1998). *What Men Want.* NY: HarperCollins Publishers Inc.

Straight from the Cougar's Mouth:

"Having a guy of my own? Fulltime? That would be exhausting."

"I was married for four years when I cheated on my wife. It was with someone at work.... She gave lots of attention and told me how much she wanted me, and really made me feel like a god. It's hard to resist that when you go home and the only thing you talk about at home are bills and when I'm planning to cut the grass."

~ Douglas, 37, who's now divorced, in David Zinczenko (2006). *Men, Love & Sex*

16 • A final word...

If you think this book has been mostly about the sexual needs of men in relationships, then you are correct. When a woman enters into a relationship with a man, she must understand that his needs will be different from hers, but if she wants that relationship with him, she will have to adapt to his needs. In a good relationship, of course, he will adapt to hers as well. It is when needs are not being met that relationships go south.

Ann Landers, the late advice columnist from many years ago, made famous a brief, to-the-point question in response to her many readers who desperately wanted to know if they should divorce their husbands. She wrote:

Would you be better off with him or without him?

No one can answer this question but you.

Every relationship has its problems and only the people involved can decide whether it's working well enough for them.

In 1973, the English pediatrician and psychoanalyst D. W. Winnicott coined the term, "the good enough mother," which described the qualities of an average mother who tended to the needs of her children in very ordinary, not extraordinary, ways. His message was that a woman did not have to be a *perfect* mother to raise healthy children. She just had to be "good enough" to meet their most basic needs adequately.

If we apply the same logic to husbands and boyfriends, perhaps we can see our way to accepting the "good enough husband" or "the good enough boyfriend" in place of the perfect husband or boyfriend that every woman dreams of. In every couple's life there will be many trials down the road that will test their determination to stay together – serious physical illnesses or infirmities, financial distress, mental or psychological deterioration to name just a few. Is it possible that you have a "good enough partner" to see you both through the long haul?

Perfection is very hard to find in this world. Perhaps Winnicott was right when he focused on just "good enough." By accepting people with their shortcomings, we are not giving them a free pass to act with impunity; instead we are recognizing their humanness and pledging to work with them to improve not only their behavior but our own in response to theirs.

Again, only you can make this determination. It is hoped that this book will enable you to look more clearly at the relationship you have and, if possible, make it "good enough" for both of you.

Ask Yourself:

- Is it possible that he's not where I think he is at this very moment?
- Would he lie to me or withhold some facts to keep me in the dark?
- Does he seem to like it when I make plans to go away with friends or family for a couple of days?
- Have I been as good a partner as I could be?

Straight from the Cougar's Mouth:

"It's not over till it's over. Do something! But do it calmly and with intelligence. Drama will only drive him away. If your relationship means something to you and you can save it, you'll be glad you did."

All contents ©2011 by Susan Anderson

ONE LIFE PUBLISHING